James Monroe

United States Presidents

James
Monroe

Series Consultant:
Don M. Coerver, professor of history
Texas Christian University, Fort Worth, Texas

Wendie C. Old

E **Enslow Publishers, Inc.**

44 Fadem Road   PO Box 38
Box 699   Aldershot
Springfield, NJ 07081   Hants GU12 6BP
USA   UK

Library of Congress Cataloging-in-Publication Data

Old, Wendie C.
    James Monroe / Wendie C. Old
      p. cm. — (United States presidents)
    Includes bibliographical references (p. 117) and index.
    Summary: Traces the life and career of the fifth president, whose
Monroe Doctrine proclaimed opposition to further European control
in the western hemisphere.
    ISBN 0-89490-941-X
    1. Monroe, James, 1758–1831—Juvenile literature. 2. Presidents—
United States—Biography—Juvenile literature. 3. United States—
Politics and government—1817–1825—Juvenile literature.
    [1. Monroe, James, 1758–1831.] I. Title. II. Series
    E372.043 1998
    973.5'4'092—dc21
    [B]   97-43699
                                            CIP
                                          AC

Printed in the United States of America

10 9 8 7 6 5 4 3 2 1

Illustration Credits: Courtesy of Independence National
Historical Park, p. 45; Courtesy of the Portrait collection, Prints
and Photographs Division, Library of Congress, Washington, D.C.,
pp. 37, 48, 94, 99, 109; The National Archives, Washington, D.C.,
pp. 41, 53; Prints and Photographs Division, Library of Congress,
Washington, D.C., p. 55; Photograph by Wendie C. Old, pp. 20, 22,
39, 100; Reproduced by Enslow Publishers, Inc., p. 85; Reproduced
from the Collections of the Library of Congress, pp. 6, 11, 59, 69,
76, 97, 106; Washington Crossing State Park, Pennsylvania
Historical and Museum Commission, p. 28.

Source Document Credits: The National Archives, Washington,
D.C., pp. 14, 33, 60, 70, 71, 98; Prints and Photographs Division,
Library of Congress, Washington, D.C., p. 9.

Cover Illustration: National Portrait Gallery, Smithsonian
Institution.

Contents

This portrait of President James Monroe was painted by Gilbert Stuart in 1817.

1

WASHINGTON, D.C., IS ATTACKED

The British are coming! The British are coming! Almost forty years earlier, at the beginning of the American Revolutionary War, these words were shouted by Paul Revere, as he made his famous ride from Boston to Lexington, Massachusetts. Now, in 1814, the words were ringing out again.

British warships had begun to patrol the east coast of the new United States during the War of 1812. By 1814, the ships had invaded the Chesapeake Bay. No one knew where they planned to attack. Perhaps they were headed to the port of Baltimore, Maryland.

Secretary of War John Armstrong assured President James Madison that Baltimore would be their target. But Secretary of State James Monroe disagreed. He urged the secretary of war to prepare a defense strategy for Washington, D.C. Monroe suggested that men be stationed at places around the capital to watch for an attack. These men could send a warning to the nation's leaders. Armstrong refused to consider this proposal.

On August 20, 1814, the British landed on Maryland soil. However, as James Monroe had predicted, they were not headed for Baltimore. Instead, the British troops advanced upon the American capital. Monroe personally led a scouting party. The British Army advanced, meeting no resistance.

Monroe helped organize the defense of nearby Bladensburg, Maryland, to the east of Washington. Seven thousand Virginia militiamen faced the invaders at this crossroads.[1] However, the Virginians panicked and ran after only sixty-six of their men had been shot.[2]

As the British moved closer to Washington, Monroe hurried to the State Department. He ordered all United States government records and documents moved. These were sent to a safe place in Leesburg, Virginia. Among the papers that were moved were the original Declaration of Independence, the Articles of Confederation, the original Constitution, and many of George Washington's letters.

On August 24, the British marched into Washington, D.C. This was their chance to destroy the seat of the American government. They easily fought off the small group of defenders, and set fire to the government buildings, one by one.

The citizens of Washington fled south and west,

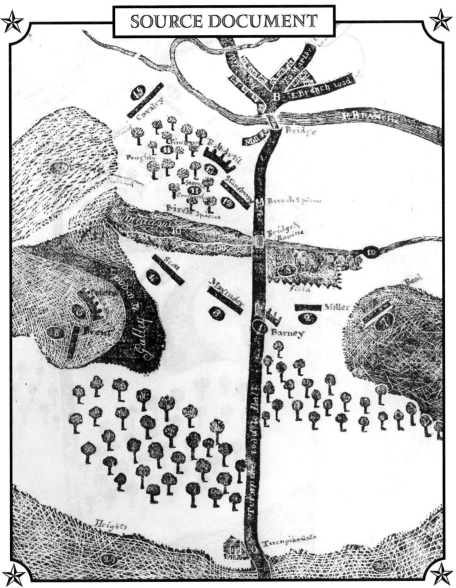

A sketch of the attack on Washington, D.C., from the notebook of a British soldier. The notebook was published in England soon after the War of 1812.

away from the invading army. They took their precious possessions with them on carts. They did not know that British general Robert Ross had ordered his troops not to damage private homes.

The first lady, Dolley Madison, personally oversaw the loading of the carts from the President's House (it was not yet called the White House). Among the things she saved from the invading army was the now-famous huge standing portrait of George Washington, painted by Gilbert Stuart. It had hung in a place of honor in the President's House for years. (The etching of President Washington's head on the one-dollar bill used today is copied from this painting.) She made sure it was carefully packed in the horse-drawn carts.

President and Dolley Madison fled west into the countryside. When British troops reached the President's House they found the dining-room table still set with food for twelve people. The soldiers immediately sat down and enjoyed the dinner. Then they piled all the furniture in the middle of the room and set fire to it.

Many of the Madisons' family possessions were ruined when the President's House was burned. All of the major government buildings in Washington, D.C., were burned. The only public building not gutted was the Patent Office. Dr. William Thornton, clerk in charge of patents, convinced the British that the items stored there were private property. Thornton knew about General Ross's orders not to destroy private property.[3]

Many of the empty homes in the capital city were

An etching of the President's House after being burned by the British in 1814. The building was gutted, and smoke damage shows above the windows.

actually looted by American servants who were left behind in the city, not by British troops. In addition to this destruction, a strong windstorm toppled some poorly built buildings and damaged others. In any case, when the British were finished with Washington, they turned to attack Baltimore, Maryland.

Because of Secretary of War John Armstrong's poor handling of war matters, President Madison fired him and turned the job over to Monroe. From September 27, 1814, through March 1815, James Monroe served the United States as both its secretary of state and its secretary of war.

A peace treaty with Great Britain was ratified on February 17, 1815. By that time, everyone in the United States viewed James Monroe as the perfect choice to be the next president of the United States.

2

VIRGINIA YOUTH

Four of the first five presidents of the United States came from the colony of Virginia. Thomas Jefferson was born in the mountains in western Virginia. George Washington, James Madison, and James Monroe were born on what is called the Northern Neck of Virginia. This is a narrow strip of land in the eastern part of the state between the Potomac and the Rappahannock rivers.

Washington's birthplace lies near the eastern tip of the Northern Neck. James Madison was born nearby while his mother was visiting her parents. He grew up in the foothills of Virginia, where he became a friend of Thomas Jefferson's.

James Monroe is the third president born there. His birthplace is just a few miles west of Washington's.

The Monroes had lived in Virginia since their ancestor, Andrew Monroe, settled there in 1650. Like the Washingtons, the Monroes were of the gentry—people who owned land. The Washingtons owned more than six thousand acres of land. However, James Monroe's father, Spence, owned only five hundred.

Spence Monroe added to his small plantation's income by working as a carpenter and builder. In the colony of Virginia a person could be a carpenter and still be a gentleman—although he would remain at the lower end of the social scale. In his autobiography, Monroe described his father as a "worthy and respectable citizen possessed of good landed and other property."[1] This included the slaves who worked the land and took care of the house.

As a builder, Spence Monroe met other Virginia architects such as the Welshman, James Jones. In 1752, Spence courted and married Jones' daughter, Elizabeth, who was known as Eliza by her family and friends. Unlike most women of that period, she was well educated. James Monroe described his mother as being ". . . a very amiable and respectable woman . . . a good wife, and a good parent."[2]

Spence Monroe brought Eliza back to his two-story frame house set in virgin forest near the source of Monroe's Creek. Within the next twelve years they had five children.

Elizabeth, the oldest and the only daughter, was born in 1754 and named after her mother. The oldest

The signatures of the first five presidents of the United States. Washington, Jefferson, Madison, and Monroe were all from Virginia. John Adams, the second president, was born in Massachusetts.

son, James, was born on April 28, 1758. Three more boys soon followed: Little Spence, born the next year, died while still a young boy. Andrew came next, followed by Joseph Jones Monroe in 1764.

By the time James was born, George Washington was twenty-six years old. On occasion he visited James's father. His tales of surveying the wilderness and fighting in the French and Indian War always enthralled the Monroe children.

James and his brothers and sister, along with the slaves' children, grew up roaming the plantation and the nearby forest. Elizabeth learned to manage a household by helping her mother. James learned plantation management from his father.

James was a normal, active boy. His enthusiasm for riding, hunting, and farming continued throughout his life. He learned early in life to use a gun. In those days a gun was useful for protection from wild animals, plus a way to add meat to a family's diet. His mother prepared delicious pies from the squirrels, pigeons, ducks, geese, and the other game James shot.

When James was eleven, he became one of twenty-five boys attending the local Campbelltown Academy. There James received a solid foundation in the classics from Parson Archibald Campbell. James was good in math and Latin. He also learned to respect the ideals of loyalty, honesty, honor, and devotion.

John Marshall, who would one day be Chief Justice of the Supreme Court, was James's fun-loving friend and kept school from being too much of a grind. The two boys would walk together down Parson's Lane to school, laughing and arguing. Each carried his books under one arm and a gun slung over his shoulder.

Both excelled in the running contests held at Parson Campbell's school, but Marshall was the fastest. The boys began calling him "Silverheels" because all they saw of him in their races was his heels flashing by.

While James was busy studying the government of ancient Rome, the tension between Great Britain and its colonies in North America was growing. To the north of Virginia, in Boston, Massachusetts, people protested the new tax on tea. On December 16, 1773, some Boston colonists disguised as American Indians dumped a load of imported tea into the harbor. News of the incident raced through the colonies. Soon it was being called "the Boston Tea Party."

The British immediately closed Boston Harbor to trade. This ruined the business of Boston merchants who depended on goods arriving by sea. The other colonies heard this news and responded.

In the colony of Virginia, the House of Burgesses met in the capital city of Williamsburg. The House of Burgesses was the local lawmaking body that ruled Virginia under the royal governor, a representative of the British king. It was made up of colonists who owned property elected by all the colonists who were gentry. The laws they made and upheld were British laws.

This group drafted a resolution supporting the

Bostonians. The Burgesses also voted to boycott, or refuse to buy, English imports. In addition, they sent letters to the other colonies asking for a combined meeting of representatives of all the British colonies to be held in Philadelphia.

This Philadelphia meeting took place in September 1774 and became the beginning of the Continental Congress. It drew thirteen of the separate British colonies on the continent together for a single purpose for the first time. Canada did not join them. The Continental Congress continued to meet and discuss common concerns for many years.

James's father, Spence, died early in 1774. James's mother's brother, Judge Joseph Jones, who was one of the influential men of the Virginia colony, helped James execute the will. Jones was a friend of George Washington and other important men in Virginia and a member of the House of Burgesses. He lived a few hours' ride to the west by horseback, in the town of Fredericksburg. Through the years, the judge brought James to the attention of the wealthy members of the ruling men in the colony.

For the rest of his life, James depended on the judge's sound practical advice. He also relied on the judge to help him support his younger brothers and make certain the boys finished their education.

With the settlement of his father's estate safe in Judge Jones's able hands, James Monroe traveled south to Williamsburg to enroll in the College of William and

Mary in June 1774. His preparation in Latin and mathematics was excellent. The college immediately enrolled him in upper-level classes.

His roommate, John A. Mercer, became James's life-long friend. Both were from backwoods plantations. Together they set out to explore life. In Williamsburg, the world of fashion and politics whirled around them. News from the home country of Great Britain arrived here first, as did news from the other colonies.

Taverns and shops lined the sides of the mile-long Duke of Gloucester Street. The Virginia House of Burgesses stood at the opposite end of the street, facing the college.

Early in 1775, delegates of the Virginia House of Burgesses met at Richmond. This was the first meeting of the Burgesses to take place away from the British royal governor in Williamsburg. Here they discussed the decisions of the First Continental Congress. It was at this meeting that delegate Patrick Henry pushed for action against Great Britain, proclaiming, "Give me liberty, or give me death."[3] This action was risky. Henry knew full well that if the colonies ever rebelled against Great Britain and failed, that he would be among the rebels who would be killed.

Every town in the colonies seethed with conflicting opinions. People who supported the king and Parliament were called Tories. People who supported the decisions of the Continental Congress of the combined colonies called themselves Patriots.

The students at William and Mary were swept up in this political excitement. James Monroe bought a rifle and joined the groups drilling on the town green, right in front of the governor's house. The royal-appointed governor could see the town militia practicing to use their arms to defend themselves against the king's soldiers. It was a threatening sight.

The town militia's gunpowder and arms were stored in a hexagonal brick building at the end of the green. It was called the Powder Horn. During the night of April 20, 1775, Governor John Murray, Earl of Dunmore, ordered the British marines stationed on the schooner *Magdalen* in the James River to invade the Powder Horn and remove all the gunpowder.

This action infuriated the people of the colony. Militia from other towns marched on Williamsburg, demanding that the governor return the powder. The royal governor offered to pay for the gunpowder, but he never returned it. Patrick Henry accepted the payment and returned to Richmond.

It was hard to stick with studying. Every week, news from the other colonies was creating excitement in Williamsburg. On April 29, people there learned of the battles of Lexington and Concord in Massachusetts. The Massachusetts colonists had defeated the British king's army stationed in Boston.

Monroe read about it in the *Virginia Gazette,* which said: "The Sword is now drawn, and God knows when it will be sheathed."[4]

The Powder Horn in Williamsburg stored the town militia's gunpowder and arms. British governor Dunmore removed the gunpowder in an unsuccessful attempt to stop the colonists from rebelling against British rule.

In June, Governor Dunmore called a session of the House of Burgesses at Williamsburg. They were to discuss important news from overseas. Great Britain's new prime minister, Lord Frederick North, had tried to stop the rebellion in the colonies with a peace offer.

The discussion grew so violent that the royal governor feared for his family's safety. He withdrew his boys from William and Mary and sent them with his wife to live aboard one of the British warships in the James River. He joined his family on board and never returned to Williamsburg. For the next several years, Governor

Dunmore's ship sailed around Chesapeake Bay and up and down Virginia's rivers.

The Virginia Burgesses refused British prime minister Lord North's peace offer. Thomas Jefferson, now a member of the Burgesses, helped draft Virginia's response. The response was called the Virginia Resolutions and Jefferson took them to the Second Continental Congress, then meeting in Philadelphia.

On June 24, 1775, twenty-four men, including James Monroe, invaded the governor's palace. They seized 230 muskets, 301 swords, and 18 pistols, plus ammunition from the palace, and placed them in the Powder Horn.

A Committee of Public Safety took over governing the colony of Virginia in place of the royal governor. Meanwhile, the Continental Congress in Philadelphia appointed George Washington Commander-in-Chief of the Continental forces. Washington took command of the army at Cambridge, Massachusetts, overlooking Boston, on July 3, 1775.

Governor Dunmore kept issuing decrees and orders from shipboard. His attempts to rule Virginia were mostly ignored. However, late in 1775, he ordered the cities of Falmouth and Norfolk to be burned for resisting his rule, and these orders were successfully carried out by soldiers aboard the British ships.

By spring of 1776, James Monroe had officially joined the Third Virginia Infantry Regiment. He was only seventeen. Monroe was six feet tall, quite strong, an excellent horseman, and a fine shot. His hair fell in unruly waves. The large nose on his plain face was offset by wide-set eyes. These eyes and his warm smile made men of all sorts feel at ease.

A total of thirty men from William and Mary joined the militia. These included Monroe's roommate, John Mercer, his friend, John Marshall, and three of the professors. As more of their countrymen joined, the three friends were made second lieutenants.

The group trained hard at Williamsburg during the spring and summer. General Andrew Lewis, who had fought successfully against American Indian uprisings, commanded them. He instilled discipline and drill.

On May 15, a convention of Virginia representatives

The governor's palace in Williamsburg, Virginia.

met in Williamsburg. They declared the United Colonies free and independent states. They pulled down the British flag from over the House of Burgesses, replacing it with the new Continental Union flag.

Patrick Henry was elected the first governor of the new independent state on June 29.

At long last, Monroe's regiment received orders to join the fight against the British. The Third and Ninth Virginia regiments moved to join Washington's army in the northern colonies. All the officers wore short-fringed cotton hunting shirts—the same summer uniform General George Washington wore in battle.

Seven hundred Virginia officers and men reported to Washington's headquarters on Manhattan Island on September 12. They brought with them a deadly weapon practically unknown in New England—the Virginia rifle. The secret of making this rifle was brought to America by German settlers in the Shenandoah Valley of Virginia. It was more accurate than any gun currently being used by the Continental Army. Throughout the war, this type of gun was also known as the Pennsylvania rifle and the Kentucky rifle, depending on where it was made. German rifle makers had settled in all three areas.

Most of the Continental Army still used muskets. A rifle used round bullets just like the musket did. However, special spiral grooves inside the rifle barrel turned the bullet. Gravity and air pressure tended to push a musket bullet away from its target. The rifle's spinning bullet flew faster and straighter. Riflemen hit their target more often. For this reason, British soldiers called the American rifle "the Widow and Orphan Maker."[5]

General Washington badly needed these guns and men. The hard fight of the Revolutionary War lay ahead of them all. Second Lieutenant James Monroe was ready.

3

WAR and PEACE

A s eighteen-year-old James Monroe fell asleep that first night on Manhattan Island, he could hear the British cannons booming across the Hudson River. The American Army camped in the countryside of the island, in an area which is now called Harlem. The men were north of the small city of New York, then confined to the southern tip of Manhattan. The rest of the island was farmland.

On September 16, 1776, the British invaded Manhattan Island. They landed near modern-day East Thirty-fourth Street. General Washington had stationed Connecticut militia there. The Connecticut militia took one look at the invaders and ran without firing a shot.

The British moved north to meet Washington's force in Harlem. Here Monroe and the Third Virginia

Regiment guarded the southern flank of Washington's army. They stationed themselves on the hills of Harlem Heights near what is 110th Street today. This small regiment held off nearly fifteen hundred British until reinforcements arrived. The Battle of Harlem Heights was one of the few battles of the early part of the war in which the Americans forced the British to retreat. General Washington praised the men in Monroe's regiment for their bravery.

Washington continued to fight defensive battles. His army was not disciplined. He could not always trust his soldiers to stay and fight. Instances like the one with the Connecticut militia were common.

Lord William Howe led the British force. Howe's men slowly pushed Washington's army off Manhattan Island. By October 26, Washington had retreated north to White Plains, New York. None of Monroe's men were killed in the Battle of White Plains on October 28, 1776. They captured thirty-six British and killed twenty.

General Howe moved his troops west of the city, into New Jersey. Washington followed. Then late in the fall, Washington's army retreated across New Jersey. The British pursued them. Gunfire was exchanged by both sides, but there was no real battle.

By the time Washington's men reached Newark, two thirds of them were sick. Only two hundred men were left in Monroe's regiment. Some soldiers had simply walked off, returning to their homes. All were poorly fed and inadequately clothed. Many did not have decent foot coverings. They slogged onward over muddy roads through the bitter November weather.

Monroe was a member of the rear guard in Newark as the American troops fled across the Delaware River, to Pennsylvania, by boat. The British could not follow because the Americans had taken every boat for thirty-five miles around.

Howe settled his troops for the winter in Princeton, Trenton, and other nearby New Jersey towns. Hired soldiers from other countries, called mercenaries, fought alongside the British troops. Among these were Hessians from a small kingdom in Germany. Howe placed the Hessian troops in Trenton.

Washington held his troops on the other side of the Delaware River in Pennsylvania. At sunset on Christmas day, in the middle of a snowstorm, he began ferrying them back across the Delaware to New Jersey. They planned to attack the Hessians in Trenton by dawn on December 26, 1776. The German troops should be groggy from celebrating Christmas with lots of food and drink, the Americans reasoned.

Monroe was part of the advance party. His regiment guarded the road, preventing anyone from warning the British. Several New Jersey farmers plus a volunteer doctor named Riker joined the American troops.

The cold snowstorm had turned to sleet. Somehow a warning message managed to reach the commander of the Hessians. He put it in his pocket without reading it and continued to play cards in his warm quarters.

Emanuel Leutze's famous painting, Washington Crossing the Delaware, *shows Washington and his men fighting broken ice and sleet. Monroe was painted holding the flag. Actually, Monroe and his men had crossed the prior evening, before the rest of the troops.*

The Americans were upon them before they knew it. In the middle of the battle, Lieutenant Monroe led an attack down a street guarded by two brass three-pounder cannons. The Germans worked frantically to fire them before both the men and the cannons were captured by the Americans. The Germans did succeed in getting off at least one blast before being overcome by the Americans.

Several men were wounded. Monroe was one of them. Blood pulsed from his shoulder from a cut artery. He might have bled to death if Dr. Riker had not been there to sew up the wound quickly.

Monroe spent the next three months recuperating at a farmhouse in Bucks County, Pennsylvania. The rest of the army wintered over in Morristown, New Jersey.

Monroe was promoted to the rank of captain for his act of bravery. However, there were no men available for him to form a new regiment.

On November 20, 1777, Monroe was appointed aide-de-camp to General William Alexander, Lord Stirling. Being an aide was not a cushy job. Aides kept records and delivered messages. They stayed close to the commanders during a battle. Many were wounded or killed.

In December, General Howe moved the British troops into Philadelphia for the winter. The American soldiers settled into nearby Valley Forge.

Many individual European soldiers had volunteered to help with the Americans' battles. During this winter encampment, Monroe forged friendships with officers of his own rank from both Europe and America. These friendships broadened Monroe's knowledge of the world and its customs.

Among his European friends was Marie Joseph Paul, the Marquis de Lafayette, a young Frenchman of great charm who spoke English well. General Washington treated Lafayette like a son. Monroe's French friends encouraged him to consider continuing his education in France after the war was over.

His new friends introduced him to philosophy, especially that of the ancient Greek and Roman Stoics. The

Stoics believed that humans become good by cultivating a reasonable outlook and not giving way to emotion. This impassive thinking appealed to Monroe, who was quite shy. Now he had a reason to present a serious face to the world.

The Roman Stoics also emphasized civic duty and social responsibility. They stressed the importance of good law, and the equal basic rights of all human beings. This ideology impressed young James Monroe. It influenced the rest of his political life.

His American friendships in camp included Alexander Hamilton and Aaron Burr, as well as John Marshall and John Mercer. Marshall had taken time off from the fighting to pass his bar exam. Now he was appointed Judge Advocate of the Army.

The young officers suffered at Valley Forge along with their men. They were exposed to body lice and illnesses such as typhus. All shared ragged clothing and sharp hunger. General Washington refused to move from his makeshift tent until all the men had log huts. Then he moved into a nearby house.

Morale was high. Washington promoted Prussian officer Friedrich Wilhelm Augustin Henry Ferdinand Baron von Steuben to the rank of major general. He kept Washington's men busy all winter long. Swearing at them in German, he drilled them until they could move as disciplined groups. In the evenings he held special classes on maneuvering and commands. When the army moved out from its winter quarters in May, it had been transformed from a ragged mob into a confident military unit.

On May 6, 1778, right before they decamped, the army at Valley Forge celebrated the recent signing of a treaty with France. Now the country of France could officially help the Americans against their old enemy, Great Britain.

Monroe's last battle with the Continental Army took place at Monmouth, New Jersey, on June 28. His scouting party discovered the British moving to reform their battle line to hit the American Army on the right. Monroe reported this discovery to General Washington. The general forced the British to retreat by nightfall. The Americans had won another battle.

In the fall, Monroe fell in love. Nannie Brown was a relative of Lord Stirling. However, the romance was doomed to be brief. Nannie became possessive of the shy, handsome aide-de-camp, and the couple argued about Monroe's desire to leave her while he studied in France. Before spring arrived they had stopped seeing each other.

By this time Monroe realized he would never gain command of a force. In an effort to be fair to all and not appear partial to men from his home state, Washington was not promoting Virginians. When Monroe sought a diplomatic appointment, he was turned down. On December 20, 1778, Monroe resigned.

When he left for Virginia, he took several letters of recommendation with him. General George Washington wrote very few letters of recommendation, but his letter for James Monroe expressed the high opinion Washington held of him: "He [is] . . . a brave, active, and sensible officer . . . it would give me particular pleasure . . . to see him provided for in some handsome way."[1]

Impressed by these high recommendations, the Virginia legislature appointed Monroe a lieutenant-colonel. However, he was expected to raise his own regiment and he failed. His modest income did not allow him to pay soldiers to join his regiment.

Monroe sold the family plantation land in Westmoreland County. With the money, he moved to Fredericksburg to be near his uncle, Judge Jones. This move also improved his social and political standing.

During the war, Monroe the military man had met Thomas Jefferson the politician. The two men began a lifelong friendship that existed for close to fifty years. Now Jefferson advised Monroe to study law.

Jefferson had become the governor of Virginia and was well known as the author of the Declaration of Independence. He liked young James Monroe for the warmth of his personality, his innate goodness, and his ready response to the feelings of others.[2]

Early in 1780, Monroe reentered the College of William and Mary. It was just a five-minute walk from the governor's palace. Together with William Smut and John Mercer, Monroe read law under the guidance of Governor Thomas Jefferson. Jefferson had his students study law cases and why they were won or lost. This case method study of law was invented by Jefferson. He also assigned readings from the philosophers.

That spring Jefferson moved the Virginia state capital from Williamsburg to Richmond. Monroe dropped out of William and Mary and followed him. With Jefferson's guidance, Monroe prepared for a career in politics.

In 1782, Washington's letters of recommendation

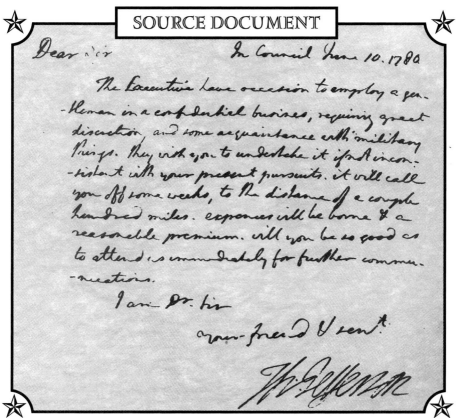

SOURCE DOCUMENT

This letter from Thomas Jefferson to his law student, James Monroe, was written on June 10, 1780.

helped get Monroe support from influential voters. (Very few people could vote in those days—only white men who owned land.) Monroe won a seat and took his uncle Judge Jones's place as a member of the Virginia House of Delegates. While there he served on the eight-man Council of State.

He also used some of the money from the sale of his small plantation to invest in land in the new territory of Kentucky. This started Monroe's lifelong interest in the western expansion of the country.

In the fall, he was elected to the Confederation Congress in Annapolis, Maryland, as part of the Virginia delegation. He took his seat on December 13, 1783.

He roomed with Jefferson, another delegate. They studied French together. Jefferson introduced him to James Madison, and the three became great friends. They often held late-night parties where the conversation ranged from politics to horses to philosophy. When Jefferson was sent to France in 1784 to replace Benjamin Franklin as minister, Madison and Monroe continued their friendship. Monroe also inherited Jefferson's library of books and his cook when Jefferson left for France.

On January 14, 1784, representatives from nine of the thirteen states approved the Treaty of Peace with Great Britain. The Revolutionary War was officially over.

His experience as part of the Confederation Congress gave Monroe a national, rather than a state's, view of affairs. He came to the conclusion that all people should get a fair share in the benefits of a "republican" government.

Men such as Monroe, Madison, and Jefferson looked to the ancient government of the Republic of Rome as their example of good government. They called it a republican government. In this ancient system, most of the land-owning men in the country had a voice in ruling the country. (This was during the time before Roman emperors ruled Rome.)

During the recess of Congress, Monroe toured the Northwest Territory. This was the land reaching from Pennsylvania and Virginia west to the Mississippi River. It also reached north beyond the Great Lakes. Most of it was claimed by the state of Virginia. Other states contested that claim.

Despite the fact that the peace treaty gave the land of the Northwest Territory to the United States, Monroe found it still to be under British influence. He listened to the concerns of the American settlers there, telling them he would take their messages back to Congress when it next met.

In January 1785, the Confederation Congress moved to New York City. Monroe was becoming a power in Congress. He was on the most important committees and chairman of several.

During the summer of 1785, he toured Ohio and Kentucky. There he learned of the distrust the settlers had of the Confederation. Many needed to use the Mississippi River to ship their goods to market. So far, the Confederation Congress supported treaties that did not allow Americans to use the Mississippi. Monroe decided to support the cause of the western settlers. He also supported the right of Congress to regulate trade in the new country. (His proposal on this issue later became part of the new United States Constitution.)

During 1785 and 1786, Monroe worked in New York City as the head of a committee to revise Jefferson's Northwest Ordinance of 1784. (While a representative to the Continental Congress, Jefferson had proposed the division of the Northwest Territory into several states if they met certain requirements.) The revision was passed in 1787. Monroe helped insure that Jefferson's original ban on slavery in the territories remained. Monroe's addition was a clause promoting the rights of settlers to navigate the Mississippi River.

New York was a hotbed of romance. Many social hostesses were eager to entertain members of Congress. There were constant teas, musical evenings, balls, and other social gatherings. In this way, many members of Congress met and married New York City women. Twenty-seven-year-old Monroe was among them. He fell in love with beautiful, seventeen-year-old Elizabeth Kortright.

Elizabeth's father, Lawrence Kortright, was a prosperous New York City merchant who had served in the British Army before the Revolution. He remained a British sympathizer during the war. After the war, Kortright become a power in the New York City business

Elizabeth Kortright Monroe.

world. Elizabeth's brother still served in the British Army. Her grandfather owned a large amount of land in the northern half of Manhattan Island.

Many of Elizabeth's society friends thought she would be marrying beneath her station. However, Monroe's friends thought he had made a good choice for a wife. They had a quiet wedding on February 16, 1786. They immediately left for the countryside of Long Island for a quiet honeymoon. From the beginning, the two formed a close bond. Every separation during their lifetime was painful to them.

Elizabeth was a tall beauty with raven hair and blue eyes. Her education had trained her to be a graceful political hostess. She presented a cold reserve in public. However, in private she became a devoted wife and a good mother. Their first child, Eliza Kortright Monroe, was born that December.

When his session of Congress ended, Monroe decided to retire from politics and become a lawyer. The couple settled in Fredericksburg. In October, he was admitted to the bar of the Courts of Appeal and Chancery. This allowed him to practice law.

The Confederation Congress governing the Confederation of States was not working out. It had very little power to keep the states together. It could not tax them. The Articles of Confederation they had signed had formed the colonies into a country of loosely banded states each with its separate laws, not a united country under one law.

The James Monroe Museum built on the site of his old law office in Fredericksburg, Virginia.

In 1786, a group of men met in Annapolis, Maryland, to organize a convention to reform the Articles of Confederation. The convention would be held in Philadelphia.

When Virginia chose delegates to the Philadelphia meeting in 1787, Monroe was not chosen. He was bitterly disappointed.[3] He felt that he should have been included because of his important work in the Continental Congress. No one else knew the problems of the western settlers like he did. Knowing that fellow Virginians George Washington and his friend James Madison were attending made him feel even worse.

The meeting in Philadelphia did not revise or reform

the Articles of Confederation. Instead it threw the entire set of Articles away and created a new document—the United States Constitution.

While the Constitutional Convention met, Monroe was again elected to the Virginia House of Delegates. He participated in the 1788 state debate over ratifying the new Constitution.

Monroe held a moderate view about the document. Although he approved of most of it, he found fault with certain parts. For instance, this new Constitution would create a strong centralized national government. It was possible that a national government might squash the states' right to rule themselves.

Monroe wanted amendments and a Bill of Rights to be added to the Constitution to insure basic freedoms like those of religion, speech, and the press (the publishing and broadcasting of news). He also favored the direct popular election of the president and senators.[4]

Therefore, Monroe allied himself with Patrick Henry's group. It was called the Anti-Federalists because they opposed the adoption of the Constitution. The Federalists supported the new Constitution.

Washington and Madison led the fight for the adoption of the new Constitution. It passed, 89 to 79 in Virginia. After it was adopted, Monroe loyally supported the Constitution. However, he still worked to amend it.

Monroe sent letters to minister Thomas Jefferson in France, keeping him informed about the debate. Jefferson's return letters reflected his active mind. As

This etching from a painting of 1786 shows Monroe's friend Thomas Jefferson as minister to France.

thoughts bubbled to the surface, he quickly dashed them off in letters to his friends. In contrast, Monroe's letters reflected his own slow, careful thinking. He often rewrote and revised these letters several times before sending them off.

In the fall of 1788, both Madison and Monroe ran for the same seat in the United States House of Representatives. Madison ran as a Federalist. Monroe ran as an Anti-Federalist. Madison won by three hundred votes. Despite their political battle, the two remained friends. This would be Monroe's first and last defeat in an election.

The next year, Monroe was able to exchange some of his Kentucky lands for a plot of land and a house in Charlottesville, Virginia. At last he would be able to live near his friends Jefferson and Madison. However, after he moved, he discovered his new eight hundred acres would not grow crops well. He needed to continue working as a lawyer to help pay his bills.

In April 1789, George Washington became the first president under the new Constitution.

Just before Christmas of 1789, Jefferson returned from France. The three friends, Jefferson, Madison, and Monroe, were able to celebrate Christmas together. Jefferson would not return to France. Washington had appointed him to be the first secretary of state. Soon Monroe would follow his two friends into the new national government.

4

DIPLOMAT

In 1790, James Monroe was elected to the United States Congress as one of the two senators from Virginia. By this time, the thirty-two-year-old Monroe had grown to resemble his uncle, Judge Joseph Jones. He was serious, reflective, and slow to come to a conclusion. However, the obvious high quality of his conclusions eventually earned him the respect of quicker-thinking men.

People liked Monroe. He could be serious and modest—almost shy. However, he attracted people with his genuine warmth and lack of malice. He made everyone around him feel at ease.[1] His tactfulness, warmhearted-ness, and patience in human relations helped him succeed in politics.

Monroe had hesitated before deciding to become a

senator. He needed to be more financially secure before returning to public service. However, his wife pointed out that the temporary capital of the United States was now located in Philadelphia. For the first time since their marriage four years ago, Elizabeth could visit her relatives who lived there.

Monroe easily defeated the Federalist candidate. He served four years in the Senate. He joined Representative Madison in supporting Secretary of State Jefferson against the policies of Secretary of the Treasury Alexander Hamilton.

Hamilton worked to create a strong central government with strong powers. However, Jefferson disagreed. He believed state powers should be stronger. President Washington valued the advice of both Hamilton and Jefferson.

The conflict between Hamilton and Jefferson continued for several years. President Washington usually found himself leaning toward Hamilton's Federalist views. Hamilton's creation of a national bank developed industry and prosperity. Hamilton's taxes raised money to support government expenses. In Congress, Senator Monroe and Representative Madison fought against Hamilton's proposals.

Secretary of State Jefferson grew tired of President Washington's always agreeing with Hamilton. Finally, early in 1793, near the end of Washington's first term, Jefferson quit.

Despite President Washington's wish, opposing

In 1790, James Monroe served in the Senate in the temporary capital city of Philadelphia. This building is Independence Hall, where Congress met.

political parties developed, their philosophies centering around Jefferson and Hamilton.

Jefferson's party was led by Madison and Monroe. They supported rule by the states and their people. They wanted a weak central government. Since this type of government was called a republic, they called their new political party Republicans. These Jeffersonian-Republicans were actually the start of the modern Democratic party.

Hamilton's party called themselves Federalists. They supported a strong federal (central) government. Monroe's old friend, John Marshall, supported the Federalists.

Jefferson never made speeches to gain supporters. Instead, he wrote letters to his friends from his estate, Monticello, in Virginia. His friends then sent these letters far and wide.

Monroe spent so much time on Jefferson's mountaintop home of Monticello, helping to build his political party, that he looked around for a place nearby to build a home for his own family. In 1793, he bought thirty-five hundred acres south of Charlottesville, on the same mountain range as Jefferson's. Monroe began building a home, and Jefferson helped design it.

In April 1793, President Washington issued a Proclamation of Neutrality. This was to keep the United States out of the war between France and Great Britain. In it he advised the states to remain friendly with both sides (neutral in the conflict).

At first Senator Monroe supported Washington's Proclamation of Neutrality. Soon he changed his mind. He feared letting the president have the right to proclaim neutrality.[2] Another president might then logically claim the right to do the opposite—to declare war. Monroe felt only Congress should have the right to declare war.

Monroe's opposition failed. In 1794, Congress passed a neutrality law. Another item Monroe opposed was the creation of a standing army in peacetime.

Monroe pushed to open up the Senate sessions to the public. Before this, the general public was not allowed to attend Senate debates. In 1794, Congress adopted Monroe's motion to change this rule. This is why everyone today has the right to sit in the balcony and watch Congress at work.

Despite the bloody revolution going on in France, Monroe was still more pro-French than pro-British. In 1794, President Washington appointed him minister to France. Monroe, his wife, and eight-year-old daughter, Eliza, spent two years there.

The president had hoped that a minister in sympathy with the French would smooth out the relations between the two nations. Monroe began at his first event in Paris, France, by praising France highly. This caused the United States secretary of state to send a reprimand, reminding Monroe that the United States was officially neutral. Monroe should only make neutral official statements.

Miniatures of James Monroe and Elizabeth Kortright Monroe painted by Louis Sené while Monroe was minister to France.

The French common people had rid themselves of their king during the French Revolution. However, the democratic government they established soon had degenerated into a "Reign of Terror." The Committee of Safety took over the rule of the country. Many people were imprisoned. Most of these were the aristocrats who had ruled the country with the king. Some of these prisoners were killed by hanging. Others had their heads cut off by the sharp blade of the guillotine, a machine designed specifically for beheading.

Monroe's old friend, the Marquis de Lafayette, an aristocrat, had participated in several battles of the French Revolution. One of them was the storming of the Bastille, a fortress where political prisoners were kept. When the Bastille had been destroyed, the marquis had even sent its key to George Washington as a symbol that the two revolutions (American and French) were working toward the same goals—freedom for the citizens and the establishment of a republic.

However, during the Reign of Terror, the French government turned on all aristocrats—even the ones who had aided their cause. Many aristocrats attempted to flee France. Lafayette did not. He was arrested and sent to prison in Germany. His wife and two children were imprisoned near Paris.

Elizabeth Monroe learned Lafayette's family would be put to death. If Minister Monroe said anything, it would look as if America was interfering in French internal affairs. However, his wife could help on a personal level.

On the very day Lafayette's wife was to be beheaded, Elizabeth Monroe drove to the prison. She demanded to see Lafayette's wife and son. After a brief visit, Elizabeth announced she would be coming back the next day to visit them again. When the authorities realized Lafayette's family had powerful friends, they canceled the French woman's execution. Soon thereafter the Lafayettes were released and allowed to join the marquis in Germany.

In February 1795, Monroe convinced the French to release every American still held in prison. This group included the fiery American writer Thomas Paine. During the American Revolutionary War, Paine had written pamphlets criticizing the king of Great Britain.

However, this time Paine had been imprisoned for supporting a king. He had protested when the French cut off King Louis XVI's head.

Paine was sick. Monroe allowed him to recover in the American minister's residence. When Paine recovered, he attacked President Washington for being so slow in getting him released. The president then blamed Monroe for failing to prevent this personal attack.

The last straw came over the news of John Jay's treaty with Great Britain. John Jay was minister to Great Britain just as James Monroe was minister to France. Both men had the duty to negotiate commercial treaties with the nation they were visiting.

President Washington and his Federalist government expected Monroe to support Jay's new commercial treaty with Great Britain. They expected him to defend it against French objections. Monroe did not. There was no way he could because he did not know what was in it. Jay had refused to tell Monroe. The French suspected the treaty favored Great Britain over France.

When he was finally informed, Monroe discovered the French were right. As an Anti-Federalist, Monroe could not support this Federalist treaty. He did not tell the French his personal thoughts about the treaty, however.

The treaty was unpopular in America as well. Although it was a major commercial agreement that recognized the new United States to be as a partner in trade, everything favored the British. It did not settle the issues of seizures of ships and men. It did not settle the boundary dispute between the state of Maine and Canada. It did, however, postpone war with Great Britain. Therefore, the Senate ratified it and President Washington signed it.

The French eventually learned the contents of the treaty through other means. They declared that it put America on the British side. The French immediately recalled their minister who was stationed in America. Now France and America were no longer allies.

Monroe protested this withdrawal. A break between the two countries could only make Great Britain stronger.

President Washington did not blame Jay's treaty for France's anger at the United States. Instead, he blamed Monroe for failing to convince the French to accept the treaty. He immediately recalled Monroe from France.

The recall notice was signed on August 22, 1796. There was a delay before it was sent across the Atlantic to France. Monroe did not receive it in France until November. He suspected the notice might have been purposely delayed to prevent him from returning to America before the next presidential election.[3]

Why was he recalled? President Washington's reason was that Monroe was not properly representing the interests of his nation or government.[4] Charles Cotesworth Pinckney was appointed minister to France in his place. (The French refused to receive him.)

Monroe wrote Madison that he would not take his family on the stormy sea in the winter. He would wait for better weather, taking his family to visit other parts of Europe.

Jefferson and Madison wrote back, telling Monroe about the presidential campaign. Vice-President John Adams was running for president as the candidate of the Federalist party. Thomas Jefferson was running as the Jeffersonian-Republican candidate.

Jefferson and Adams had been friends in the Continental Congress. They had worked together on the writing of the Declaration of Independence. However, beginning with the bitter campaign of 1796, they were political enemies.

The Constitution had not provided for two enemies campaigning against each other. In November 1796, John Adams won—by three electoral votes. Jefferson came in second. According to the Constitution, this made Jefferson vice-president under Adams.

Many people thought Jefferson would refuse to serve under his enemy. However, Jefferson recognized that the people had elected him. He would serve in the office he had won.

Monroe arrived back in Philadelphia on June 27, 1797. He was angry and bitter about his treatment by the American government.[5] He immediately wrote to Secretary of State Pickering asking why he had been recalled. After ten days, Pickering replied that the president did not need to supply any reason for recalling a minister.

By September, the Monroe family had moved back

An etching of John Adams, president of the United States, 1797–1801.

to Charlottesville, Virginia. On December 2, 1797, James Monroe published a written defense of his actions in France. He called it, "View of the Conduct of the Executive in the Foreign Affairs of the United States, Connected with the Mission to the French Republic, During the Years 1794, '5 & '6." "View" was almost five hundred pages long.[6] It included every possible official paper of his years as minister to France. Public response was mixed.

Federalists counterattacked immediately. Even President Adams criticized this treatise. Monroe began to write responses to his critics, but he changed his mind and decided not to.

In Europe, the French military leader, Napoleon Bonaparte, was leading French forces to victory in Italy. French ships were capturing American ships. The English Navy was defeating French forces on the seas. If Monroe were to defend his treatise, it might now seem as if he were defending France against the interests of his own country.

The year 1798 was a dark and depressing time for James Monroe. He gave up politics and returned to farming and practicing law. At this time, however, farms were bringing in less and less income. Monroe tried to sell some of his land to raise money to support his family. The price of land was too low to help. He had few law clients. Monroe had to mortgage his farms to pay for the high cost of transporting his furniture home from

France. It was during this period that he fell deeper and deeper into debt.

However, Virginians refused to let him retire. The legislature nominated him for governor of Virginia in 1799. He was elected three times to serve one-year terms as governor.

Three other events happened in 1799. First, his only son, James Spence Monroe, was born.

Second, his house on the mountainside near Monticello was finally completed. The Monroe family moved up the winding, steep mountain road into the new one-story, six-room frame house. They called their new home on the mountainside "Highland."

A view of James Monroe's home, Highland. It was designed by Thomas Jefferson and built by Monroe.

Third, George Washington died in December at his Virginia home, Mount Vernon.

On August 3, 1800, Governor Monroe received word about a planned slave uprising. During the night, almost one thousand slaves were prepared to murder all the whites on their plantations. Then, they would advance on Richmond and set fire to the city. They hoped to capture the armory full of guns and ammunition.

Monroe called out the Virginia militia. The fires that were lit in town quickly died out in a hard rainstorm. One hundred slaves were arrested.

Most of the white population pitied the rebelling slaves. Governor Monroe issued an official statement: ". . . among the causes for the slaves' unrest were 'the contrast between free Negroes and the slaves,' the inadequacy of the existing patrol laws, and 'a growing sentiment of liberty in the minds of the Blacks.'"[7]

Vice-President Jefferson suggested that the rebels be sent out West instead of being punished. There they could establish a settlement of free African Americans. Monroe preferred sending them to South America. However, twenty-five were tried and executed. The rest were pardoned and sent back to their owners.

During this time of extreme unrest, Elizabeth carried their small son from doctor to doctor. He had fallen sick with whooping cough and never recovered. James Spence Monroe died on September 28, 1800.

Monroe kept his grief private, shared only with his

wife and young daughter. He hid his anguish in public by focusing his energies on politics.

In 1800, he and Madison led the Jeffersonian-Republicans in the fight to elect Thomas Jefferson president of the United States. Aaron Burr, a political power in New York, also ran as a Jeffersonian-Republican. President John Adams and Thomas Pinckney were Federalist candidates.

It was a bitter battle. The final vote was Jefferson 73, Burr 73, Adams 65, and Pinckney 64.[8] Jefferson and Burr had tied.

Everyone expected Burr to accept the vice-presidential spot. He refused. For the first time, the law stating that the House of Representatives of Congress must decide in case of a tie came into effect. After thirty-six ballots, Jefferson finally won a clear majority.

In 1802, during Monroe's third year as governor of Virginia, newly elected President Jefferson visited him. He requested Monroe return to France as a special ambassador—his title would be Envoy Extraordinary and Minister Plenipotentiary.

France owned a huge chunk of land in the middle of North America called Louisiana. It ranged from the port of New Orleans in the South to Canada in the North. The eastern border was the Mississippi River. The Rocky Mountains bounded its western edge.

Jefferson had already sent instructions to the American minister to France, Robert R. Livingston, to negotiate free access to the Mississippi River for

Americans. Could Monroe, with his vast French experience, help him settle the deal?

In early 1803, the Monroes sailed to France. They brought along sixteen-year-old Eliza and their new baby, Maria Hester. James Monroe had been authorized to buy the port of New Orleans, Louisiana, and the neighboring lands. This would insure permanent access to the Mississippi River for Americans.

Napoleon Bonaparte had graduated from merely being head of the French Army to ruling all of France. At present there was a lull in the war between Great Britain and France. Napoleon needed money to resume the war.

The two negotiators, Monroe and Livingston, were authorized by Congress to offer Napoleon from $2 million to $10 million for the land.

Napoleon made a fast decision. He would get rid of his American lands. This would leave him free to concentrate on the European field. Quickly he offered back: The United States could not have New Orleans and the small patch of land around it. But, if the price were right, the United States could purchase the whole of Louisiana. What price would the United States offer?

As a dictator, Napoleon could make instant decisions affecting his whole country. However, Livingston and Monroe came from a democratic country. They were supposed to get approval from Congress before making major decisions like this purchase. On the other hand,

Congress was all the way across the ocean. It would take three or four months to travel there, reach a decision, and travel back by ship. Napoleon wanted a decision immediately.

Livingston and Monroe discussed this dilemma. Should they accept Napoleon's offer? If they did, would Congress and the people of the United States back their decision? They examined their directions from the president. Jefferson's orders were to be flexible. They were to get the best deal possible for the United States.

An artist's rendition of the negotiations for the Louisiana Purchase. From left to right, Monroe, Livingston, and Napoleon's foreign minister, Charles Talleyrand.

Therefore, the two American representatives negotiated a price with Napoleon and his foreign minister, Charles Talleyrand. Finally, they agreed on $15 million for all of Louisiana.[9] The deal was struck on May 2, 1803. It would be called the Louisiana Purchase.

Many of Jefferson's and Monroe's enemies accused them of loving the French. That could be the only explanation why they would offer to pay so much for such worthless real estate. President Jefferson stood by the action of his ambassadors.

Jefferson brought the completed treaty before Congress. There was a long and bitter debate. It ended

SOURCE DOCUMENT

A map of the present United States showing the outline of the territory included in the Louisiana Purchase.

in 1803 with Congress approving the treaty with Napoleon by a huge majority.

Most Americans reacted to the news that their country had doubled in size with shock, delight, and astonishment. Some reacted with dismay.[10] The money that had been spent on this purchase would increase the national debt by millions of dollars.

Suddenly the United States of America was larger in size than most of the major powers in Europe.

5

MORE ON THE WAR OF 1812

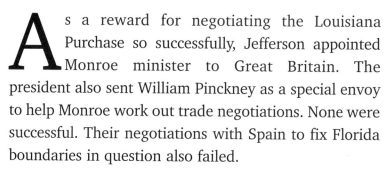

As a reward for negotiating the Louisiana Purchase so successfully, Jefferson appointed Monroe minister to Great Britain. The president also sent William Pinckney as a special envoy to help Monroe work out trade negotiations. None were successful. Their negotiations with Spain to fix Florida boundaries in question also failed.

In 1806, the two finally negotiated a commercial treaty with Great Britain. This treaty attempted to end the conflict between the two countries over shipping.

However, when the negotiating team sent the treaty to the United States, Jefferson and his secretary of state, James Madison, rejected it. The treaty had failed to deal with one of the main conflicts between the United States and Great Britain—the issue of impressment, or the search and seizure of enemy ships and citizens. Jefferson refused to present what he considered an unacceptable treaty to Congress for ratification. This action wounded Monroe deeply.[1]

Great Britain continued to stop American ships. British captains continued to impress (kidnap) American citizens from those ships and force them to work on British ships. Eventually this conflict would lead to war between the two countries, but not yet.

Back in the United States, President Jefferson called for an embargo (or ban) against trading with Great Britain. As a measure to prevent war, this embargo worked. However, it caused much economic hardship. Tobacco, without a good market, became as worthless as weeds. The United States had cut off its major customer.

The Monroes returned to the United States, arriving home on December 13, 1807, after a stormy voyage. When they disembarked from the ship, people noticed and talked about the new clothing style worn by five-year-old Maria Hester.

The child's dress came to between her knees and ankles. Her legs were covered down to her shoes by pantaloons. This fashion allowed Maria Hester the freedom to romp around after her spaniel. Up until now, small children—even the boys—wore long dresses that made it difficult to move about. Word spread quickly about this new French fashion. Soon almost every child in America wore pantaloons.

A quick visit to Washington, D.C., the nation's new capital, proved useless for Monroe. President Jefferson had no other plans to use him in his government.

When the Monroe family returned to Virginia, some members of his party discussed the possibility that Monroe run for president. Monroe assured them that if he was chosen as the party candidate, he would be willing to run.

However, when all the state representatives of the Jeffersonian-Republican party met, they wound up proposing a different candidate—James Madison. George Clinton of New York ran as his vice-president. The Federalists ran Charles Cotesworth Pinckney for president with Rufus King for vice-president.

In the end, Madison and Clinton won easily. There was no mention of a post for Monroe.

Monroe resented this snub. He and Madison stopped visiting each other. Monroe did not invite Madison and his family to the marriage of his older daughter Eliza to George Hay in September 1808. This conflict between his two young friends saddened Jefferson.[2]

Eventually Monroe was offered the governorship of the new territory of Louisiana. However, Monroe refused to be exiled to that "wasteland." Monroe wanted to be secretary of state. He turned his back on politics and tended to his farms.

The embargo had ruined the market for tobacco. Monroe changed to raising grains. He amazed his neighbors by spreading plaster of paris (made of lime) on his fields. The resulting bumper crop convinced others to use this new farming method.

In April 1810, Monroe was elected to the Virginia House of Delegates. In May he visited Washington, D.C., and talked to President Madison. There they patched up their differences.

On January 16, 1811, Monroe was elected governor of Virginia again. He held this office for only three months. President Madison finally dismissed his first secretary of state, Robert Smith, and asked Monroe to fill the post.

Monroe was hesitant. He wondered if it would be a problem that he often held views of foreign policy that differed from Madison's. The president assured him their past differences should not be a problem. Monroe moved into his new post on April 5.

President Madison's wife, Dolley, welcomed the cool, reserved Elizabeth Monroe to Washington. Dolley Payne Madison was a famous Washington hostess, outgoing and bubbly. She had served as President Jefferson's hostess at the President's House since Jefferson was a widower. Therefore, when her husband became president, she was already comfortable in that role.

Monroe's first problem as secretary of state was the European war between Great Britain and France. Both countries were attacking all neutral ships, including those of the United States.

War seemed likely, but with whom? British ships had attacked American ships right outside New York Harbor in sight of land. The French fleet bragged of burning American ships at sea.

In Congress, groups of "war-hawks" led by Henry Clay, John C. Calhoun, and Richard M. Johnson called for war—against both countries. In December an army bill was passed. In addition, the House adopted a resolution that allowed merchant vessels to arm themselves. This would allow them to resist attack by foreign ships of war from any nation.

Monroe pushed for an alliance with Great Britain. America had more family ties with Great Britain. Plus, he saw it as the more powerful country. President Madison pushed for an alliance with France, remembering how France had helped the Americans during the Revolutionary War.

In a letter, Monroe explained to a friend that war ". . . could not do us more injury than the present state of things. . . ." and ". . . [war] would give activity to our infant manufactures, which would soon be able to shut the door on British industry."[3]

On June 18, 1812, both houses of Congress passed a declaration of war against Great Britain. In the United States, it was called the War of 1812. Congress had no idea that two days earlier in London, the British Parliament had passed an act that gave in to most of the American demands for peace except for the issue of impressment. However, there was no way to send messages instantly across the Atlantic Ocean. It still took more than a month for a ship carrying the news to reach the other side.

By that time, the United States had already attacked Canada. The Americans were using the excuse of war to attempt to expand their territory to the north. In addition, General Andrew Jackson moved a force into Spanish-held Florida on the southern border. The attacks on Canada failed. The Florida situation took much longer to be resolved.

On the other hand, the American Navy outclassed any vessel the British could spare to fight them. The frigates *Constitution, President,* and *United States* had been built with double-layer hulls. British shot seemed to bounce right off them. This earned them the nickname of "ironsides." They were not really metal ships. Metal-clad ships were not built until the 1860s.

Most of the British Navy had not yet arrived in North America. It was still involved in Great Britain's war with Napoleon.

In the fall, James Madison easily won reelection as president for another four-year term.

All the armed forces complained about Secretary of War William Eustis. In December 1812, he resigned. Monroe became acting secretary of war while continuing as secretary of state. He was now fifty-four years old. Monroe's experience observing the commanders in the Revolutionary War now proved useful.

However, the Federalists in the Senate (mostly New Englanders) prevented his appointment from becoming permanent. They objected to giving so much power to another Virginian. Monroe supported Madison's search for another secretary of war. As soon as one could be found, Madison promised to give Monroe a field command. (He never got one.)

The British proceeded to blockade America's coasts. This strategy ruined American trade—especially in New England. Americans were unsure just where the British would land their forces.

The year 1813 brought more unsuccessful American military actions in Canada. In Europe, the British defeated the French again and again.

Madison found a new secretary of war in February 1813. John Armstrong from New York had also served in the American War of Independence. However, he had a reputation for lying and being difficult to work with. He constantly fought with Secretary of State Monroe. He tried to take charge of the war itself, which also brought him into conflict with the Commander-in-Chief, President Madison.

A British fleet entered the Chesapeake Bay in the spring. It attacked several cities along the shore of the bay. This is when Monroe urged Armstrong to prepare to defend Washington, D.C., suggesting men be stationed around the city to watch out for attack. Armstrong refused to consider the idea. He insisted the British were headed for Baltimore, instead.

Americans had more success on the Great Lakes. Naval officer Oliver Hazard Perry's ships destroyed the

British fleet on Lake Erie in September. They now controlled the Detroit frontier region. Gradually Perry pushed the British eastward.

The low point of the war for the Americans came in 1814. The British had defeated the French. Now they could concentrate on the American front. They moved more men and material across the Atlantic Ocean.

A British fleet controlled the Chesapeake. On August 20, the British landed and advanced on the American capital. Monroe helped organize the defense of nearby Bladensburg, Maryland, to the east. It failed. It was then that Monroe ordered all State Department records and documents sent to a safe place.

On August 24, 1814, the British marched into Washington, D.C. The citizens of Washington, including President and Dolley Madison, fled. All of the major government buildings in Washington, D.C., were burned. In this way the British troops took revenge for

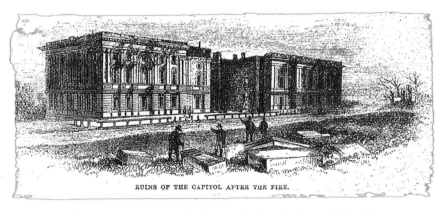

RUINS OF THE CAPITOL AFTER THE FIRE.

An etching of the U.S. Capitol after the British burned Washington, D.C., in 1814.

SOURCE DOCUMENT

The Star-spangled banner

STAR SPANGLED BANNER IN HANDWRITING OF FRANCIS SCOTT KEY

A handwritten copy of the lyrics to Francis Scott Key's "The Star-Spangled Banner," which became the national anthem in 1931.

the American burning of public buildings in Toronto, Canada.

The British then turned to attack Baltimore, Maryland. There they met with stiffer resistance. Fort McHenry defended the harbor. An American lawyer, Francis Scott Key, had boarded a British ship to conduct an exchange of prisoners. He was supposed to free American prisoners aboard the ships in exchange for freeing British soldiers captured on land. However, the British refused. These American prisoners aboard the ships had seen and heard the British plans for the attack on Baltimore. As a result, Key was also held prisoner during the battle at Baltimore. Key wrote down in the form of a poem his feelings about seeing the American flag still waving over Fort McHenry at dawn. He and the other prisoners were released after the battle. The poem was eventually published, passed from friend to friend, and finally put to music. In 1931, the United States officially adopted this song, "The Star-Spangled Banner," as its national anthem.

On September 27, 1814, Madison temporarily replaced Armstrong with Monroe as secretary of war. Monroe held this position until March 1815. He continued to be secretary of state as well.

The war along the Canadian border continued to favor the Americans. A British force invaded New York State. The American fleet on Lake Champlain defeated the British on September 11, 1814. Captain Thomas MacDonough won the naval battle of Lake Champlain

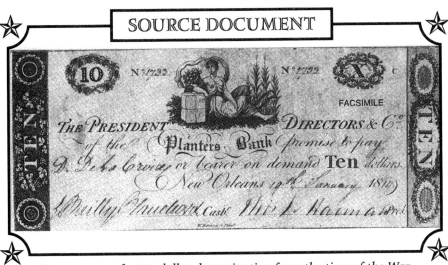

SOURCE DOCUMENT

Paper money of a ten-dollar denomination from the time of the War of 1812.

in Plattsburg Bay. The British invasion had been repulsed. The British Army retreated back into Canada.

These two setbacks persuaded the British government to seek peace. American and British diplomats began negotiating in Ghent, a city in the Low Country of Europe.

At this time, Monroe and President Madison saw disaster after disaster looming. The nation faced economic bankruptcy. New England threatened to secede from the Union of American States.

The Hartford Convention met in Connecticut in December 1814 through January 1815. In the end, this group finally decided not to break away from the Union. However its members suggested a number of constitutional amendments to restrict federal power.

In Ghent, the British learned of their defeats in Baltimore and the north. They gave up the idea of demanding American territory. With the American economy bankrupt, the Americans gave up the idea of demanding that the British respect their neutral rights.

The Treaty of Ghent was signed in Europe by both powers on December 24, 1814. It simply supported the conditions in existence at the beginning of the war. On the other hand, it did prove the United States had an equal and respected place in world affairs.

However, the British military strategy outlined in the fall of 1814 had been three-pronged. There was also a southern attack planned to take place at New Orleans to block the Mississippi River.

Before the news of the signed peace treaty could reach the United States from Ghent, the southern British force attacked New Orleans. General Andrew Jackson defended the city. In January 1815, he defeated the attacking British forces. Two thousand British were wounded or dead. On the American side there were fewer than one hundred casualties.[4]

As a result, Americans learned about the British defeat at New Orleans before they learned of the treaty. The country felt that the war had ended in triumph. A wave of nationalist feeling swept across the country.[5] The United States Senate ratified the treaty unanimously on February 17, 1815.

To the north, the United States saw that Canada would never join their Union. However, Jackson's invasion of the Floridas showed that the Spanish hold on their Latin American colonies might be loosening.

At the end of this war, Monroe was seen to be the man of the day. He had been secretary of state. He had also been secretary of war. Therefore, he was seen as the man responsible for its successful conclusion.

He was also the choice of President Madison and ex-President Jefferson to be the next president of the United States. The country wholeheartedly agreed.

6

PRESIDENT OF THE UNITED STATES

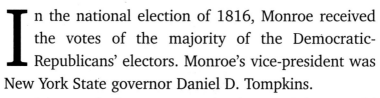

I n the national election of 1816, Monroe received the votes of the majority of the Democratic-Republicans' electors. Monroe's vice-president was New York State governor Daniel D. Tompkins.

This was the last time a Federalist candidate would run for the presidency. Rufus King of New York only carried three states. The Federalist party was dead.

By the time James Monroe was elected president of the United States, his hair was almost entirely gray. His good humor still showed in his wide-set, blue-gray eyes and dimpled chin. Like many other older men, he no longer wore up-to-date clothing.

He was the last president who had fought in the Revolutionary War. During this war, men wore breeches, stockings, and their tricornered hats cocked to one side of the head.

By the time Monroe became president, the fashion had changed. Most men wore long trousers and frock coats. However, Monroe still wore the type of clothing that had been popular when he was a young man. He wore silver buckles on his shoes, silk stockings, knee breeches, and ruffled shirts, all of excellent quality. As a result, he was called the "Last of the Cocked Hats."

Monroe was also the last of the "Virginia Dynasty" of presidents. Washington, Jefferson, Madison, and finally Monroe had worked together to create a new type of government. Now, with the end of the War of 1812, they had proved that the United States of America was a strong republic, newly respected among the nations of the world.

The Capitol was still being rebuilt after the huge fire. Congress was meeting in a much smaller building. There was no place where both Houses could meet together to observe the inauguration of President Monroe. Therefore, it was decided to hold the first out-door ceremony.

Monroe took his oath of office on Tuesday, March 4, 1817. His good friend, John Marshall, now Chief Justice of the Supreme Court, administered it on a platform on the East Portico of the Capitol. In his inaugural address, Monroe promised to ". . . adopt such arrangements as are indispensable to the support of our independence, our rights and liberties. . . ."[1]

One of the best-known portraits of James Monroe. It was painted during his first term in office by Charles Bird King. The etching made from it was reproduced in many books, journals, and prints.

While the President's House was still being refurbished from the ravages of the fire of 1814, the new president and his family lived at the Octagon House at Eighteenth Street and New York Avenue. The final touch to the President's House was a coat of white paint. From then on, it would be called the White House.

The Madisons had lived in the fire-damaged President's House. They replaced damaged pieces with some secondhand furniture. Now Congress passed a bill to help pay to refurnish the White House.

Monroe was plagued with overdue bills. He also needed to cover the expenses of entertaining at the White House. The money allocated by Congress for this activity helped, but it would not be enough. Presidents were expected to use some of their own fortune. But Monroe did not have the private income most of the previous presidents had enjoyed. Also, because he was in public office, he could not work as a lawyer to earn the extra income required to cover his expenses. His debt grew ever larger.

However, the Monroes did own fine furniture from France. Monroe sold this to the United States for use in the White House. The money helped pay off some of his debt. During the next few years, more items were purchased under the direction of Elizabeth Monroe. In time, the furnishings of the White House equaled those of any palace in Europe.

For shy Elizabeth Monroe, it was difficult to succeed Dolley Madison as first lady. Dolley had been a great political hostess for years. Her parties were famous. She also regularly visited everyone who was important in Washington. By the end of her husband's term of office, Dolley was quite exhausted.

Elizabeth Monroe had not been in good health for some time. Because of her weakness, she decided that the hostess of the White House would not make the first visit to other Washington ladies. Instead, the ladies of Washington, D.C., must now call on the wife of the president first and introduce themselves. This shift in policy made her unpopular. For some time, the ladies of Washington ignored the first lady.

The Monroes escaped from the pressures of Washington to their country estate at Oak Hill in Loudoun County, Virginia. This estate, thirty-five miles away, was where their daughter Eliza and her husband, George Hay, lived.

Monroe offered the post of secretary of state to John Quincy Adams, son of ex-president John Adams. In a letter to Jefferson, Monroe explained that he made this appointment, "in order to offset talk in the North that the high offices were only for Virginians."[2] The Adams family came from Massachusetts. He made a good choice: John Quincy Adams is considered one of the greatest secretaries of state this country has ever had.

The men Monroe chose for his Cabinet came from all sections of the country. He offered Henry Clay, the leader of the western representatives, a choice of any of the remaining Cabinet positions. However, Clay refused. He had wanted to be secretary of state.

One of Monroe's first acts as president was to tour the United States. He traveled as far north as Portland, Maine, and as far west as Detroit, Michigan. In Boston, a Federalist newspaper, the *Columbian Centinel*, coined a phrase that later was applied to Monroe's entire presidency. The paper said Monroe's visit there began an "Era of Good Feelings."[3]

In 1817 these good feelings spread. The Rush-Bagot Agreement with Great Britain was signed. This eliminated fortifications on the Canadian-American border and removed warships from the Great Lakes. This border between British-held Canada and the United States became the longest unguarded border in the world.

Monroe understood that roads must be built to tie the east with the west. New waterways would also merge different parts of the country together into one nation. However, Monroe did not believe the money for such projects should come from the federal government. It would be better if the states paid for them directly. He supported the construction of the Erie Canal, which began on July 4, 1817, because state money was used.

Conflict arose on the southern border. Escaped African slaves and Seminole tribesmen from the Spanish-owned Florida area raided settlements in Georgia. They killed many people. Appeals to Spain to stop this action were ignored. President Monroe asked General Andrew Jackson to deal with the problem.

In November 1817, the first Seminole War began. Seminole bands attacked European settlements in Florida. Fearing these attacks would spread to the southern United States, Monroe sent in General Jackson to help settle things. He destroyed Seminole villages. He overthrew the Spanish governor. He killed two British citizens who had incited the Seminoles.

Many people, including Secretary of War John Calhoun, urged that Monroe reprimand Andrew Jackson. By overthrowing Spanish rule, Jackson had exceeded his authority. He was ordered to move out of Florida. However, Jackson's military action had convinced Spain that the United States could capture Florida any time it wished.

Many territories became states during Monroe's terms of office. The first one was Mississippi. It was admitted on December 10, 1817, as the twentieth state.

Each time a state was admitted, the American flag changed. A star was added into the blue field. Another stripe was added to the red and white stripes. By this time, the flag of the United States was huge. For example, the flag Francis Scott Key saw in 1814 waving from Fort McHenry in the Baltimore harbor boasted fifteen stars and fifteen stripes. (This flag is now in the Smithsonian Institution in Washington, D.C.)

If many more stripes were added, the flag would become too large to wave. On April 4, 1818, the official flag of the United States was established. Only thirteen stripes would be kept—one for each of the original colonies. However, stars would be added to the blue field to indicate the number of states in the Union. The blue field was enlarged by one star for the first time when Illinois was admitted as the twenty-first state on December 3, 1818.

The northern border of the United States was finally determined by the Convention of 1818. This agreement between the United States and Great Britain drew a line from Minnesota to the Rocky Mountains.

Within the United States various tribes of American Indians still claimed independence. The Chickasaw tribe signed a peace treaty with the United States on October 19, 1818. This treaty redefined the tribe's rights and the boundaries of their land.

The United States had gained French-held lands with the Louisiana Purchase. However, Spain continued to claim vast territories on the southern, southwestern, western, and northwestern borders of the United States.

Secretary of State John Quincy Adams negotiated with the Spanish minister, Luís de Onís. On February 22, 1819, the Adams-Onís Treaty was signed. Spain gave Florida to the United States. The new southern boundary of the United States continued along the Sabine River. This left what is modern Texas in Spanish territory.

Spain also gave up any claim to the Oregon territory which reached from Spanish California to Russian

Alaska. Finally, the United States reached from sea to shining sea.

It would be several years before the United States Congress ratified the treaty. In addition, the northern border of this Oregon Territory would have to be negotiated with Great Britain.

The United States should have been enjoying peace and prosperity. Unfortunately, bad business practices plunged it into a financial panic in 1819. Banks failed. Land speculation in the West lost people money. European imports competed with domestic goods. This caused an economic depression worse than the one under Jefferson. It lasted until 1821.

Monroe traveled through the southern states to examine firsthand the areas hardest hit by the Panic of 1819. He asked Congress to raise tariffs on European goods. This made the European goods in the stores more expensive, causing people to want to buy American-made goods instead. He also asked Congress to reduce government spending.

There was no problem in admitting Alabama as the twenty-second state on December 14, 1819. So far, Congress had admitted one state promoting slavery for every state that forbade slavery in its territory.

However, a real conflict erupted when Congress considered the next two states requesting admission.

7

THE MISSOURI COMPROMISE

T he individual states' attitudes about slavery were becoming farther and farther apart. The southern states had long growing seasons. They developed a strong agricultural economy. Growing food and grain is labor-intensive. Many hands are required to tend the crops. Many people must gather and store the crops. The South grew dependent on large groups of slaves to do this work.

The northern states had short growing seasons. They developed industries instead. Industries used machines to do the work. Although they needed hands to tend the machines, they did not need as many. The northern states could hire cheap labor to work in their factories.

By the turn of the century, most of the northern

states had outlawed slavery within their borders. In the South, slaves were considered part of the landowner's property. Virginia was a southern state. Most of the presidents of the United States, including Monroe, had owned slaves.

When the Louisiana Territory was opened to settlers, they brought their property with them. Southern settlers brought their slaves. Northern settlers brought their antislavery ideas with them. These two conflicting interests fought it out in the new territories.

The Federal Convention of 1787 declared all states and territories south of the Mason-Dixon line and the Ohio River could be slave-holding states. (The Mason-Dixon line is the boundary between Pennsylvania and Maryland. It was originally surveyed by the surveyors, Charles Mason and Jeremiah Dixon.) North of the line, slavery was abolished or would die out in a few years.

As states were added, the number of slave-holding and free states remained balanced. First, a slave state would be admitted. Then, a free state would join the Union. With the admission of Alabama in 1819, there were eleven slave states and eleven free states. That also made an equal number of senators in Congress from slave and free states.

However, many slave-owning settlers settled in the upper Louisiana Territory. They built large wheat and cotton plantations in the rich bottomlands of the lower

Missouri River. Other plantations grew on the west bank of the Mississippi, near St. Louis.

In 1818, the people in this northern territory called Missouri wished to be admitted as a state. They voted to be admitted as a slave state, even though they were north of the Ohio River dividing line. When the petition was submitted in the House of Representatives, there was much debate.

A northern congressman, James Tallmadge of New York, attached an amendment to the petition. The amendment would have ended slavery in Missouri within a generation by insisting that all slave children be freed at age twenty-five. It also forbade the importation of new slaves. The House passed the bill admitting Missouri. The Senate defeated the bill. Congress adjourned in March.

During the time Congress did not meet, the country discussed this statehood problem. Some people in the North realized the admission of Missouri would give slave states a majority in the Senate. They suggested the northern states secede (break away) from the United States if slavery were not defeated.

Other people, in the South, demanded the right to own their own property in the newly settled territories. They threatened to secede if this right were to be refused. None of them ever debated the moral right or wrong of slavery itself.

Monroe's friend, ex-President Jefferson wrote, "This momentous question, like a fire bell in the night, awakened and filled me with terror. . . . I considered it at once as the [death] knell of the Union."[1]

Meanwhile, the Territory of Maine separated from Massachusetts. It wished to be admitted as a free state into the United States.

In January 1820, Congress met again. Speaker of the House Henry Clay proposed a compromise. Missouri would be allowed to enter the United States as a slave state. However, it would be the only slave state that far north. Slavery would now be absolutely prohibited in United States territory north of latitude 36°30′. This was the southern border of Missouri. At the same time, Maine would be admitted as a free state. This would make twelve free states and twelve slave states.

The South was pleased with the compromise. They were certain the next states to be admitted—Arkansas and Florida—would be slave states. The North knew that a great expanse of the Louisiana Purchase lay north of that latitude. Eventually, even more free, northern states would join the Union.

Monroe's secretary of state, John Quincy Adams, predicted the future American Civil War when he wrote in his diary, "I take it for granted that the present question is a mere preamble—a title-page to a great, tragic volume."[2]

President James Monroe was now faced with a momentous decision. He came from a southern state. He owned slaves, himself. With the power of a veto, he could stop this whole action. Should he sign this compromise into law? Should he reflect the will of the nation? Or should he follow the will of his slave-owning home state of Virginia?

He was of two minds about signing. In fact, he had even drafted a veto message. There was a possibility Congress lacked constitutional authority to ban slavery

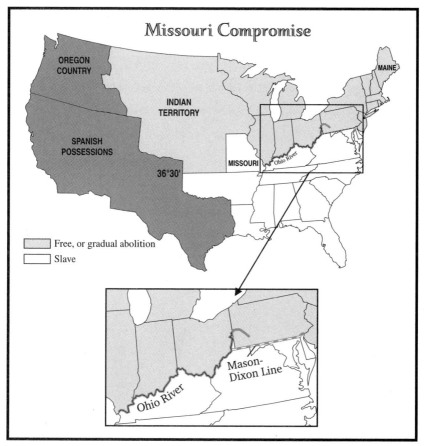

This map shows the distribution of slave and free territory as of 1820, according to the Missouri Compromise. As part of the compromise, Maine was admitted to the Union as a free state; Missouri as a slave state. Slavery was prohibited in all other territory north of 36°30´ latitude.

in the territories. However, he reconsidered. He feared a veto might cause a civil war among the states.[3]

On March 6, 1820, President Monroe signed the Missouri Compromise into law. Civil war was postponed for a while.

Maine was officially admitted as the twenty-third state on March 15, 1820. However, it took much longer for Missouri to become an actual state.

Missouri's first constitution excluded any free blacks from entering or living in the state. Antislavery members of Congress challenged this clause. Missouri could not be admitted until that had been changed.

Missouri finally became a state on August 10, 1821.

8

THE MONROE DOCTRINE

M onroe took a little break from politics in the spring. Maria Hester Monroe had the honor of being the first daughter of a president to be married in the White House. Sixteen-year-old Maria had fallen in love with her handsome cousin, Samuel L. Gouverneur. In those days it was common for cousins to marry each other.

In accord with the Monroe family's desire to keep their personal life private (and to save on the expense), the couple were married on March 9, 1820, in a quiet ceremony. Only forty-two friends and relatives were invited. Monroe put Gouverneur to work as his secretary. (The couple lived with her parents in the White House until 1822 when they moved to New York City so Gouverneur could study law.)

The Federalist party no longer existed. No other party had organized itself. In 1820, Monroe became the first (and only) president to run for reelection unopposed. Daniel D. Tompkins was again his running mate.

It seemed Monroe was now the first president to exemplify George Washington's ideal for the presidency: Monroe had the support of *all* the people of the nation, not just that of one political party.

However, when the 232 electors cast their ballots, they did not give Monroe a unanimous vote. George Washington has the record of being the only president to receive the unanimous vote of the electoral college.

One of the electors from New Hampshire—Governor William Plumer—cast his ballot for Secretary of State John Quincy Adams, much to Adams's embarrassment. Plumer was an older man and a staunch Federalist. He was tired of the country being ruled by Virginians. Plus, he simply did not like James Monroe and his Democratic-Republican policies.[1]

The subject of Florida finally settled a week before Monroe's second inauguration. President Monroe had objected to one of the original provisions of the treaty relating to Florida and the Oregon Territory.

The Spanish and Portuguese colonies in South America were declaring their independence and forming new countries. They were asking to be recognized by the other countries of the world. Spain wanted the United States to stay neutral and refuse to recognize the colonies' independence.

Monroe sent a special message to Congress on May 9, 1820, stating his views. He declared that "it [Spain's request] is . . . so repugnant to the honor and even the independence of the United States that it has been impossible to discuss it."[2]

The treaty was revised and sent back to Spain. By February 22, 1821, the final details of the treaty with Spain had been worked out.

That year, March 4 fell on a Sunday. Therefore, Monroe's second inauguration ceremony was held on Monday, March 5, 1821. It was the first time the ceremony had been postponed. The weather did not allow for an outdoor inauguration. Both snow and rain poured down on Washington, D.C.

By this time the Capitol had been repaired. Monroe took his oath of office inside the beautiful new chamber of the Hall of Representatives. Again, Chief Justice John Marshall administered the oath.

President Monroe's second inaugural address was brief. He emphasized how the American government was an improvement over all other forms of government, even the ancient Republics: "In this great nation there is but one order, that of the people, whose power . . . is transferred from them . . . to persons elected by themselves. . . ."[3]

During Monroe's first term, Elizabeth Monroe was often sick. Now her illness became worse. No one knew quite what it was. Her older daughter, Eliza, often substituted for her as official hostess of the White

Statue of Monroe's younger daughter, Maria Hester. She wore this dress to her father's second inaugural ball. The statue is on display at the Smithsonian Institute.

House. Like her mother, Eliza presented a cold, formal face in public.

Monroe cut down the number of formal receptions and dinners for congressmen and foreign diplomats. He was worried about his wife. He was also worried about the money he still owed. However, even these measures were not enough. The expense of living in Washington, plus maintaining two other homes, put him ever deeper in debt. He never accepted invitations to private homes. Many of the leaders in Washington society blamed Eliza for the reduced White House social life.

As long as the territory of Florida was in question, Monroe remained cautious in discussing the new Latin American countries that had declared their freedom from Spain and Portugal. However, once Florida belonged to the United States, he could speak.

Monroe revealed his sympathy toward the Latin American rebels in messages to Congress, despite the official United States policy to remain neutral. Monroe did this to counter Henry Clay's speeches. Clay was trying to raise opposition to Monroe and his Era of Good Feelings. He had claimed that Monroe's administration was against Latin Americans.

In March of 1822, Monroe sent word to Congress. He wanted the United States formally to recognize Mexico and the Latin American republics. A bill was immediately written and passed.

Another bill passed in that session of Congress was proposed by Henry Clay. As a representative of the western states, he thought federal money should be used to build roads and canals.

President Monroe supported improved transportation in the West. However, Monroe thought there was nothing in the Constitution that authorized the federal government to help. He felt raising funds for construction should be left up to the states.

Clay pointed out that the federal government supported trade routes in the East. The government built lighthouses and aided shipping. Why could it not support trade routes along the roads in the West? Clay's bill allowed federal money to build toll booths on the Cumberland Road. The toll money collected would pay for extending the highway westward.

When the bill finally lay on President Monroe's desk, he vetoed it. This was the only veto President Monroe used in his two terms of office.

In Europe, many of the European governments refused to recognize the new independent Portuguese and Spanish colonies in South America. Members of the European royal families, most of whom were related to each other, came up with a plan. They decided the younger sons of the Spanish, French, and Italian royal families should rule various parts of their former South American colonies.

The king of France supported the Spanish king's desire to regain control of his colonies. There was talk of France's gaining a foothold there as well. The government in Great Britain discovered this plan.

The foreign minister of England, George Canning, spoke with the American minister, Richard Rush, about this problem at the American embassy in London on August 16, 1823. Rush was pleased when he heard that the British government was against the French action.[4]

Rush asked Canning if Great Britain was willing to recognize the new Latin American countries. At this time, Canning would not commit either himself or his country. Rush made a record of each of these conversations. He sent them by sailing ship in the diplomatic pouch to the State Department in Washington, D.C. In addition, he sent for instructions.

The messages finally reached President Monroe on October 9. He discussed the situation with Secretary of State John Quincy Adams. As was his habit, he also sent letters to his friends, ex-Presidents Thomas Jefferson and James Madison. He told them his plans for handling the situation. Both agreed with Monroe that some stand should be taken about the Western Hemisphere's independence from Europe.

Beginning on November 3, Monroe and his Cabinet discussed these foreign developments. Should the United States and England make a joint declaration? Or should the United States stand alone?

Secretary of State John Quincy Adams advised President Monroe not to make a joint declaration with Great Britain. Monroe agreed with Adams that a bold statement on United States policy alone would be much more effective than to "come in as a cock-boat [small rowboat] in the wake of the British man-of-war [large fighting ship]."[5]

Threats to the new United States did not come only from Europe. The Kingdom of Russia had placed settlements in Alaska. Their claims kept pushing farther south down the west coast of the American continent—into the new Oregon Territory. The United States had to watch all sides of its country.

President Monroe decided to issue the statement as part of his annual end-of-the-year message to Congress. These messages traditionally reported on the president's activities during the past year. They also contained suggestions for future foreign and domestic policy. Monroe, Adams, and the rest of the Cabinet spent two weeks hammering out the exact wording of this year's message. In addition, they drafted notes to the various foreign governments involved in the current international situations.

On December 2, 1823, President James Monroe sent his seventh annual message to Congress. A clerk read it aloud to a joint assembly of Congress. It included the statement that ". . . The American continents . . . are henceforth not to be considered as subjects for future colonization by any European powers."[6] Monroe had no idea that he had just formulated an important American policy. He was simply responding to the times.

The important sections that came to make up the Monroe Doctrine were widely separated in this message. They were not joined together and given the

President James Monroe, standing (in old-fashioned knee breeches and stockings), with his Cabinet (in modern trousers), discussing the Monroe Doctrine.

official name of "The Monroe Doctrine" until 1853. The basic parts of this doctrine include

> The American continents . . . are henceforth not to be considered as subjects for future colonization by any European powers.
>
> The political system of the allied [European] powers is essentially different . . . from that of America. . . . We should consider any attempt on their part to extend their system to any portion of this hemisphere as dangerous to our peace and safety.
>
> With the existing colonies or dependencies of any European power we have not interfered and shall not interfere.
>
> In the wars of the European powers in matters relating to themselves we have never taken any part, . . . [and it is not] our policy so to do.[7]

The part declaring neutrality in European affairs was ignored in the twentieth century. At that time, several worldwide conflicts swept the United States into war. However, the central core of the doctrine still stands: *The countries of the Eastern Hemisphere must keep their hands off the Western Hemisphere.*

SOURCE DOCUMENT

Fellow Citizens of the Senate and House of Representatives.

Many important subjects will claim your attention, during the present Session, of which I shall endeavour to give, in aid of your deliberations, a just idea in this communication. I undertake this duty with diffidence, from the vast extent of the interests on which I have to treat, and of their great importance to every portion of our Union. I enter on it with zeal, from a thorough conviction, that there never was a period, since the establishment of our Revolution, when regarding the condition of the civilized world, and its bearing on us, there was greater necessity for devotion in the public servants, to their respective duties, or for virtue, patriotism, and union, in our Constituents.

A copy of the December 2, 1823 message to Congress which contained what later became known as the Monroe Doctrine.

President James Monroe toward the end of his presidency.

The American people overwhelmingly approved Monroe's declaration. Newspapers praised it. National spirit was at an all-time high. This ringing message had come from a modest nation whose capital had been burned by British invaders just nine years before. Yet now this nation was proposing to defend both North and South America from foreign involvement.

In the session of Congress of 1824, Henry Clay fought for what he called the American System. He proposed higher protective tariffs. He also insisted roads be improved. Some of his bills passed.

Congress invited Monroe's old French friend, the Marquis de Lafayette, to visit the United States. He landed on August 15, 1824, and began touring the country. The marquis was welcomed in every state he visited. It was a year-long celebration of friendship. Monroe wrote to Madison that Lafayette was "respected and beloved by all for his devotion to [our republican] principles."[8]

Sixty-year-old President Monroe met with him privately at Oak Hill. Lafayette went on to visit Thomas Jefferson and James Madison at their homes.

Monroe's last year in office was complicated by another issue. Southern states had originally claimed their borders reached to the Mississippi River. These states agreed they would draw their state borders

Statue of the Marquis de Lafayette presented to Monroe by Lafayette when he revisited the United States in 1824. The statue now sits in the reproduction of James Monroe's law office and museum in Fredericksburg, Virginia.

over a smaller land area, provided the federal government would help move American Indian tribes out of their territories. This would open up more land for European settlers. The state of Georgia had given up all claims to its western lands. In exchange, the federal government agreed to move the Cherokee, Chickasaw, Creek, Choctaw, and Seminole tribes out of Georgia, where settlers wanted their lands. However, the chiefs refused to sell their lands or to exchange them for lands farther to the west.

Monroe mentioned relations with American Indian tribes in his last annual message to Congress. In a special message late in January 1825, he recommended the removal of all American Indians east of the Mississippi River to western territories. When his presidency and the Eighteenth Congress's meeting came to an end, no action had been taken. This problem would be passed on to the next president.

Monroe's secretary of state, John Quincy Adams, won the election in the fall of 1824 to become the sixth president of the United States. Monroe's secretary of war, John Calhoun of South Carolina, easily won the post of vice-president.

President Monroe took no interest in the election. Elizabeth Monroe was so ill that friends thought she would die soon. He was also concerned about his ever deepening debt.[9]

9

RETIREMENT

On March 4, 1825, John Quincy Adams took the presidential oath of office. However, he had to postpone moving into the White House because the Monroe family was unable to move out. Mrs. Monroe was too sick to travel.

Three weeks later, Monroe and his family moved to his nearby estate at Oak Hill. Monroe's plans to retire at Highland, near his friends Jefferson and Madison, had to be put aside. He could now afford only one place to live. He sold Highland to help pay his debts.

Highland still exists. It was renamed Ash Lawn by the new owners. Today it is called Ash Lawn/Highland, owned and run by the College of William and Mary.

Monroe refused to sell his slaves along with the

land. He wrote in a letter that "I wish to sell [them] at private sale, in families."[1]

President Monroe retired from public office deep in debt. For years his income had not supported the extra costs of being a public servant. Each year he owed more and more money. By the time he retired, he owed $75,000.[2] This would be equal to over a million dollars in today's money.

At this time in history, retired presidents were not given a pension. There was no Social Security, either. A person was expected to support himself and his (often very large) family all the days of his life.

Monroe not only had to support a sick wife, as oldest and head of the family, he was expected to help support his brothers and their families. None of his brothers became successful in life. They continually turned to James for support.

In addition, he helped his daughters' husbands. The bad economy of the past years had reduced the income from his agricultural lands. When he tried to sell his vast land holdings to raise money, the price of land was down as well. He did not receive the true value for his property.

But he had another plan in the works to raise money. Before James Monroe retired from the presidency, he presented a bill of expenses to Congress. In this bill he asked Congress to reimburse him for $53,836.[3] This amount represented the expenses (plus interest) incurred from his post as minister in France up through the years of his presidency.

Congress considered Monroe's carefully presented accounting. It did not give him an answer until the next year. In 1826, Congress awarded him a mere $29,513. Monroe was disappointed with the payment.[4] However, he was not able to convince Congress to raise the amount by a single penny.

In the middle of the year 1826, two of the founders of the United States of America died. Both Thomas Jefferson and John Adams died on July 4, 1826—the fiftieth anniversary of the signing of the Declaration of Independence.

Monroe had worked with both men to ". . . convert the ideals of the Revolution . . . into a basic reality of American life . . . [to] serve as a model and as an example to the rest of the world."[5]

Thomas Jefferson had built the University of Virginia on the land Monroe had once owned in Charlottesville. When Jefferson died in 1826, Monroe replaced him on the Board of Regents.

Elizabeth Monroe's illness grew worse. Modern historians think it is possible that she suffered from epilepsy, which people called the "falling sickness" in Monroe's time. That year she suffered a violent seizure. She fell into the fireplace and was badly burned. She never really recovered.

Monroe continued to be active in the affairs of the state of Virginia. In 1829, he was made president of the

Virginia State Constitutional Convention. This group worked to amend the state constitution. He supported the conservative view on suffrage and slavery.

Elizabeth Monroe died the next year, on September 23, 1830. In his despair, James destroyed all of his wife's letters. Each empty room reminded Monroe of her. Finally, he decided he could no longer live at Oak Hill without Elizabeth.

Monroe sold Oak Hill and moved to New York City to be close to his youngest daughter, Maria Hester, and her husband, Samuel Gouverneur. While there, he began writing his memoirs. However, he soon became too sick to complete them.

Monroe had been suffering for several years with a nagging cough. It may have been a sign of tuberculosis. He weakened steadily during his final months of life.

In 1831, the third presidential survivor of the Revolutionary War died peacefully. He died—appropriately perhaps—on the very same day that both Jefferson and Adams did—July 4. The death certificate recorded the cause as heart failure.

A huge funeral was held on July 7 in New York City. Church bells tolled. Guns boomed from the Battery at the southern tip of the island—once for each of the seventy-three years of the president's life.

Thousands of mourners followed the gold and black hearse to the graveyard. He was buried in the Gouverneur family vault. In 1858, his body was moved to Hollywood Cemetery in Richmond, Virginia.

The home of Maria Hester Monroe Gouverneur and Samuel Gouverneur in New York City where James Monroe died.

10

LEGACY

onroe died unaware of the long-lasting effects of his Monroe Doctrine message to Congress. He died believing that adding Florida and the Oregon Territory to the United States was the major achievement of his administration.[1]

This quiet, but well-liked gentleman was the last president to have fought in the Revolutionary War. In fact, until his death, Monroe served in every war the United States fought to maintain its independence from foreign influence.

He had also participated in almost every major event that formed the new United States. He held more major political offices—both state and national—than any other American president. He had been the governor of Virginia. He had been a United States senator.

Thomas Jefferson had sent him to France to negotiate the Louisiana Purchase. This doubled the size of the country. He had been the foreign minister to three countries—Great Britain, France, and for a short time, Spain. Monroe had held two Cabinet posts at one time during the War of 1812—both secretary of state and secretary of war.

His friend, ex-President James Madison, praised Monroe's fine administrative abilities. Madison said, "His understanding was very much underrated. . . . His judgment was particularly good. . . ."[2]

Monroe's contributions to American history are still underrated by historians. His achievements have often been overshadowed by those of the presidents who served before and after him. Historians applaud the brilliance of Thomas Jefferson. They praise the generalship of George Washington. James Madison is known as the architect of the United States Constitution. The names of John Adams and his son, John Quincy Adams, are carved in history books because of their statesmanship.

James Monroe was an example of the best type of public servant, one severely needed by the new republic. He was hardworking and self-sacrificing. Ex-President Thomas Jefferson, the older friend and mentor of both Madison and Monroe, said, "Monroe was so honest that if you turned his soul inside out there would not be a spot on it."[3]

Even though Monroe owned slaves, he signed the

Eng. by A.B. Durand. from the Painting by J. Vanderlyn. in the City Hall New-York.

JAMES MONROE.

An etching of President James Monroe (with his signature) from the painting by J. Vanderlyn.

Missouri Compromise, which established states where slavery would be forbidden.

For years Monroe had supported the movement to help freed African slaves return to Africa. This movement was led by the American Colonization Society, founded in 1817. The movement had gained control of the country of Upper Guinea in West Africa. Many freed slaves agreed to settle there. However, the movement was not a complete success. Many more freedmen wished to stay in America—the country where they had been born.

Upper Guinea honored James Monroe during his last year as president. On August 15, 1824, it changed its name to Liberia. Its capital city became Monrovia, in honor of President James Monroe. It is the only foreign capital city named after an American president.

During Monroe's two-term presidency, the United States included five more states. The territories of Oregon and Florida also enlarged the country.

His 1823 message to Congress has survived as a basic principle of American foreign policy as the Monroe Doctrine, a warning to European countries to keep their hands off the Americas.

Monroe's letters all featured political topics. He wrote very little about his private life. However, he did publish several articles, all of which defended his public political actions. Right before he died, he began writing his autobiography.

Monroe succeeded in his goal to make the United

States a strong country, separate from Great Britain. The experiment in democracy was not only working, it was working well. The young country was no longer dependent on European practice and attitudes. At the end of Monroe's presidency, the United States was respected throughout the world.

His successor, President John Quincy Adams, declared that Monroe had worked ". . . strengthening and consolidating the . . . edifice of his country's Union, till he was entitled to say, like Augustus Caesar of his imperial city [Rome], that he had found her built of brick and left her constructed of marble."[4]

Chronology

1758—James Monroe is born on the Monroe plantation in Westmoreland County, Virginia, April 28.

1774—Father, Spence Monroe, dies; James enters College of William and Mary in Williamsburg, Virginia.

1775—Is commissioned a second lieutenant in the Third Virginia Infantry Regiment, September 28.

1776—Sees action at the Battle of Harlem Heights, September 16; at White Plains, October 28; and at Trenton, where he is wounded, December 26.

1777—Is promoted to major and appointed aide-de-camp to General William Alexander, known as Lord Stirling, November 20.

1778—Fights at Monmouth, June 28; resigns to enter civilian service in Virginia, December 20.

1780—Studies law under Virginia governor Thomas Jefferson.

1781—Serves on Governor Thomas Jefferson's council.
–1783

1782—Is elected to the Virginia assembly.

1783—Is Virginia's representative to the Congress of
–1786 the Confederation.

1786—Marries Elizabeth Kortright, February 16; daughter Eliza Kortright Monroe is born in December.

1787—Is elected to the Virginia House of Delegates.

1788—Serves in the state convention that ratifies the new Constitution of the United States.

1790—Serves in the U.S. Senate.
–1794

1794—Serves two years as minister to France.
–1796

1796—Is recalled from France, August 22.

1799—Is elected governor of Virginia (is later reelected twice); son, James Spence Monroe, is born.

1800—Son, James Spence Monroe, dies September 28.

1803—Daughter, Maria Hester Monroe, is born; goes to France as President Jefferson's special envoy to assist Minister Robert R. Livingston in negotiating the purchase of the Louisiana Territory; becomes minister to Great Britain in July.

1810—Serves in the Virginia House of Delegates.

1811—Is elected governor of Virginia, January 16; serves only three months; as secretary of state directs American foreign affairs during the War of 1812.

1814—Serves briefly as secretary of war, September
–1815   27 through March.

1816—Is elected president.

1817—Is inaugurated president, March 4; signs Rush-Bagot Agreement with Great Britain eliminating fortifications on the Canadian-United States border; Mississippi admitted as twentieth state, December 10.

1817—First Seminole War.
–1818

1818—Legislation establishes the flag of the United States, April 4; treaty with Chickasaw Indians, October 19; Illinois is admitted as the twenty-first state, December 3.

1819—Florida is purchased from Spain when the Adams-Onís Treaty is signed, February 22; Alabama is admitted as twenty-second state, December 14.

1820—Missouri Compromise is signed, March 6; daughter Maria is married in the White House, March 9; wins reelection with all but one electoral vote.

1821—Second inaugural address, March 5; Missouri admitted as twenty-fourth state, August 10.

1823—Monroe Doctrine is proclaimed, December 2.

1824—Capital city of Liberia is named Monrovia in his honor, August 15.

1825—Retires to his estate at Oak Hill in Loudoun County, Virginia.

1826—Becomes a regent of the University of Virginia.

1829—Is chairman of Virginia State Constitutional Convention.

1830—Elizabeth Monroe dies, September 23.

1831—James Monroe dies in New York City, July 4.

Chapter Notes

Chapter 1. Washington, D.C., Is Attacked

1. Samuel Eliot Morison and Henry Steele Commager, *The Growth of the American Republic*, vol. 1 (New York: Oxford University Press, 1962), p. 422.

2. Ibid.

3. Harry Ammon, *James Monroe, The Quest for National Identity* (Charlottesville: University Press of Virginia, 1990), p. 335.

Chapter 2. Virginia Youth

1. James Monroe, *Autobiography* (Syracuse, N.Y.: Syracuse University Press, 1959), p. 21.

2. Harry Ammon, *James Monroe, The Quest for National Identity* (Charlottesville: University Press of Virginia, 1990), p. 2.

3. Nobel E. Cunningham, Jr., *In Pursuit of Reason, The Life of Thomas Jefferson* (Baton Rouge: Louisiana State University Press, 1987), p. 32.

4. William Penn Cresson, *James Monroe* (Chapel Hill: University of North Carolina Press, 1946), p. 11.

5. C. Keith Wilbur, *Illustrated Living History Series, The Revolutionary Soldier, 1775–1783* (Philadelphia, Pa.: Chelsea House Publishers, 1997), p. 31.

Chapter 3. War and Peace

1. James Monroe, *Autobiography* (Syracuse, N.Y.: Syracuse University Press, 1959), p. 29.

2. Harry Ammon, *James Monroe, The Quest for National Identity* (Charlottesville: University Press of Virginia, 1990), p. 30.

3. William Penn Cresson, *James Monroe* (Chapel Hill: University of North Carolina Press, 1946), p. 96.

4. Noble E. Cunningham, Jr., "James Monroe," in the *Reader's Companion to American History* (Boston: Houghton Mifflin, 1991), p. 741 (online search, Infotrack search, General Reference Center, Gold, 1997).

Chapter 4. Diplomat

1. Harry Ammon, *James Monroe, The Quest for National Identity* (Charlottesville: University Press of Virginia, 1990), p. 8.

2. William A. DeGregorio, *Complete Book of U.S. Presidents* (New York: Dembner Books, 1984), p. 76.

3. Daniel C. Gilman, *James Monroe* (Boston: Houghton Mifflin, 1898), p. 67.

4. David L. Bongard, "James Monroe (1758–1831)," *The Harper Encyclopedia of Military Biography* (New York: HarperCollins, 1992), p. 517 (online General Reference Center, Gold, 1997).

5. William Penn Cresson, *James Monroe* (Chapel Hill: University of North Carolina Press, 1946), p. 154.

6. Ammon, p. 166.

7. Arthur Styron, *The Last of the Cocked Hats—James Monroe & the Virginia Dynasty* (Norman: University of Oklahoma Press, 1945), p. 223.

8. Joseph Nathan Kane, *Facts about the Presidents from George Washington to Ronald Reagan* (New York: H. W. Wilson, Co., 1981), p. 26.

9. Dumas Malone, *Jefferson and His Time, Jefferson the President—First Term, 1801–1805* (Boston: Little, Brown and Company, 1970), p. 302.

10. Daniel J. Boorstin, *The Landmark History of the American People: Volume 1—From Plymouth to Appomattox* (New York: Random House, 1987), p. 91.

Chapter 5. More on the War of 1812

1. Harry Ammon, *James Monroe, The Quest for National Identity* (Charlottesville: University Press of Virginia, 1990), p. 266.

2. Ibid., p. 273.

3. William Penn Cresson, *James Monroe* (Chapel Hill: University of North Carolina Press, 1946), pp. 252–253.

4. Reginald Horsman, "War of 1812," *The New Grolier Multimedia Encyclopedia*, 1993 CD-ROM.

5. Arthur Styron, *The Last of the Cocked Hats—James Monroe & the Virginia Dynasty* (Norman: University of Oklahoma Press, 1945), p. 333.

Chapter 6. President of the United States

1. William A. DeGregorio, *Complete Book of U.S. Presidents* (New York: Barricade Books, 1984), p. 79.

2. Arthur Styron, *The Last of the Cocked Hats—James Monroe & the Virginia Dynasty* (Norman: University of Oklahoma Press, 1945), p. 340.

3. "James Monroe, Fifth President 1817–1828," *National Geographic*, November 1964, p. 681.

Chapter 7. The Missouri Compromise

1. Samuel Eliot Morison and Henry Steele Commager, *The Growth of the American Republic*, vol. 1 (New York: Oxford University Press, 1962), p. 444.

2. Ibid.

3. William A. DeGregorio, *Complete Book of U.S. Presidents* (New York: Barricade Books, 1984), p. 82.

Chapter 8. The Monroe Doctrine

1. William A. DeGregorio, *Complete Book of U.S. Presidents* (New York: Barricade Books, 1984), p. 79.

2. Noble E. Cunningham, Jr., *The Presidency of James Monroe* (Lawrence: University Press of Kansas, 1995), p. 106.

3. DeGregorio, p. 80.

4. George Dangerfield, *The Awakening of American Nationalism, 1815–1828* (New York: Harper & Row, 1965), p. 175.

5. Thomas A. Bailey, *A Diplomatic History of the American People* (New York: Meredith Publishing Co., 1964), p. 182.

6. Samuel Eliot Morison and Henry Steele Commager, *The Growth of the American Republic*, vol. 1 (New York: Oxford University Press, 1962), pp. 459–460.

7. Ibid.

8. Cunningham, Jr., p. 171.

9. Ibid., p. 179.

Chapter 9. Retirement

1. Paula Xinis-Fishman, *Monroe On . . .* (Williamsburg, Va.: Ash Lawn-Highland Monroe Collection pamphlet), p. 32.

2. William A. DeGregorio, *Complete Book of U.S. Presidents* (New York: Barricade Books, 1984), p. 84.

3. Lucius Wilmerding, Jr., *James Monroe: Public Claimant* (New Brunswick, N.J.: Rutgers University Press, 1960), p. 83.

4. Noble E. Cunningham, Jr., *The Presidency of James Monroe* (Lawrence: University Press of Kansas, 1995), p. 184.

5. Harry Ammon, *James Monroe, The Quest for National Identity* (Charlottesville: University Press of Virginia, 1990), p. 19.

Chapter 10. Legacy

1. Harry Ammon, *James Monroe, The Quest for National Identity* (Charlottesville: University Press of Virginia, 1990), p. ix.

2. "James Monroe, Fifth President 1817–1828," *National Geographic*, November 1964, p. 679.

3. Ibid.

4. Ammon, p. 573.

Further Reading

Ammon, Harry. *James Monroe, The Quest for National Identity*. Charlottesville, Virginia: University Press of Virginia, 1971.

Bains, Rae. *James Monroe, Young Patriot*. Mahwah, N.J.: Troll Communications L.L.C., 1986.

Bosco, Peter I. *War of 1812*. Minneapolis, Minn.: Millbrook Press, 1991.

Carter, Alden R. *War of 1812*. New York: Franklin Watts, 1992.

Fitz-Gerald, Christine M. *James Monroe*. Danbury, Conn.: Children's Press, 1987.

Hanser, Richard. *The Glorious Hour of Lt. Monroe*. New York: Atheneum, 1976.

Kane, Joseph Nathan. *Facts about the Presidents from George Washington to. . . .* New York: H. W. Wilson, Co. (updated regularly).

Meltzer, Milton. *Thomas Jefferson, The Revolutionary Aristocrat*. New York: Franklin Watts, 1991.

Morris, Richard B. *The War of 1812*. Minneapolis, Minn.: Lerner Publications, 1985.

Old, Wendie C. *George Washington*. Springfield, N.J.: Enslow Publishers, Inc., 1997.

———. *Thomas Jefferson*. Springfield, N.J.: Enslow Publishers, Inc., 1997.

Phelan, Mary Kay. *The Story of the Louisiana Purchase.* New York: Thomas Y. Crowell, 1979.

Sandak, Cass R. *The Monroes.* New York: Macmillan, 1993.

Stefoff, Rebecca. *James Monroe: 5th President of the United States.* Ada, Okla.: Garrett Educational Corporation, 1988.

Wade, Linda. *James Monroe.* Hawthorne, N.J.: January Productions, Inc., 1993.

Weber, Michael. *Madison, Monroe & Quincy Adams.* Vera Beach, Fla.: Rourke Corporation, 1996.

Wilbur, C. Keith. *Illustrated Living History Series, The Revolutionary Soldier, 1775–1783.* Philadelphia, Pa.: Chelsea House Publishers, 1997.

Places to Visit

Pennsylvania

Valley Forge (just west of Philadelphia). The reconstructed winter camp of the Revolutionary War. The park is open for drive-through every day.

Washington Crossing. A reenactment of the crossing by George Washington's army is done on Christmas Day. The park is open for drive-through every day.

Virginia

Ash Lawn-Highland, Charlottesville. A 535-acre estate on the same mountain range as Thomas Jefferson's estate, Monticello. It is owned and run by Monroe's alma mater, the College of William and Mary in Williamsburg. Open every day except Thanksgiving, Christmas, and New Year's Day. For further information write to Ash Lawn-Highland, James Monroe Parkway, Charlottesville, Virginia 22902.

James Monroe Museum and Memorial Library (owned by the Commonwealth of Virginia and administered by Mary Washington College), Fredericksburg. A reconstructed building stands on the site of James Monroe's law office. Open every day except Thanksgiving, December 24, 25, 31, and January 1. For further information write the museum at 908 Charles Street, Fredericksburg, Virginia 22401.

Oak Hill, near Leesburg, James Monroe's country retreat when he was president.

Washington, D.C.

The White House. Open mornings, Tuesday through Saturday, except on some holidays and during official White House functions. Twenty-four-hour recorded information available at (202) 456-7041.

Internet Addresses

Ash Lawn-Highland, the home of James Monroe.

<http://monticello.avenue.gen.va.us/Tourism/
AshLawn/>

Colonial Williamsburg.

<http://www.history.org>

**Information about the James Monroe Museum
in Fredericksburg, Virginia.**

<http://www.artcom.com/museums/vs/gl/
22401-58.htm>

Monroe Doctrine.

<http://odur.let.rug.nl/~welling/usa/documents/
monroedoc.html>

**Political document links including the United
States Constitution and the Declaration of
Independence.**

<http://www.cs.indiana.edu/inds/politics.html>

Presidential Facts.

<http://www.usahistory.com/>

**University of Virginia, founded by Thomas
Jefferson on James Monroe's land.**

<http://www.virginia.edu/>

The White House (U.S. President articles).

<http://www.whitehouse.gov/WH/glimpse/
presidents/html/presidents.html>

Williamsburg Online.

<http://www.gc.net/wol/wol.html>

Index